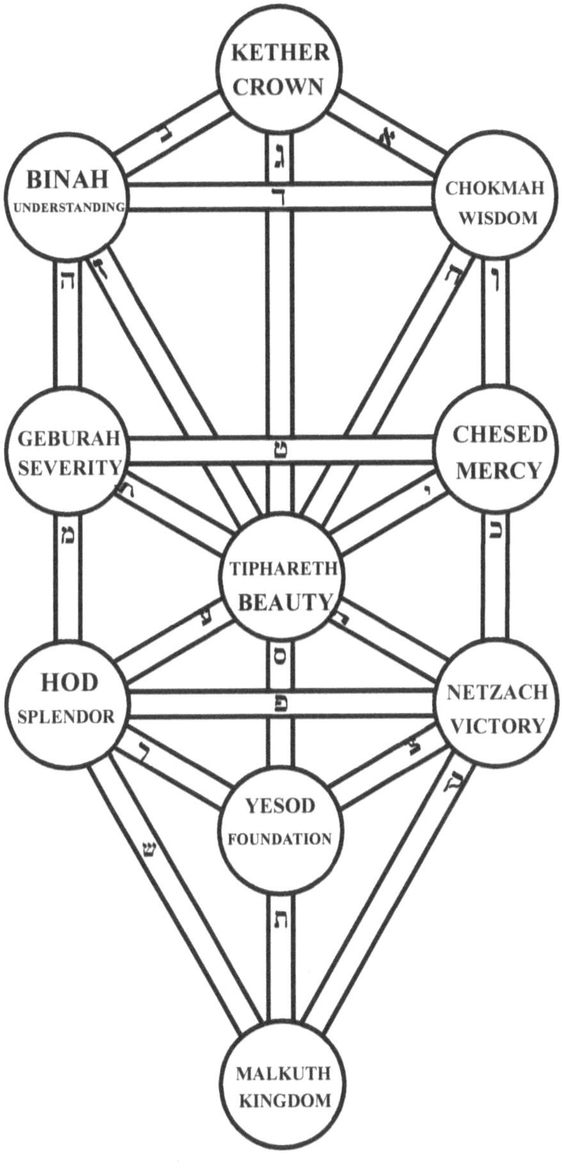
KETHER
CROWN
BINAH
UNDERSTANDING
CHOKMAH
WISDOM
GEBURAH
SEVERITY
CHESED
MERCY
TIPHARETH
BEAUTY
HOD
SPLENDOR
NETZACH
VICTORY
YESOD
FOUNDATION
MALKUTH
KINGDOM

The Hermetic Qabalah

&

The Tree of Life

Dr. Paul A. Clark

Steward of the Fraternity of the Hidden Light

The Fraternity of the Hidden Light

P.O. Box 5094

Covina, CA 91723

Copyright © 2012 Paul A. Clark

All rights reserved. No part of this book may be reproduced or utilized in any way, electronic of mechanical, including photocopying, recording, or by any information storage and retrieval system, without permission in writing from the publisher.

ISBN   978-0-9710469-1-7

Printed and bound in the United States by Lightning Source Press

Table of Contents

Introduction	1
Part I General Considerations	5
Chapter 1 The Hermetic Principles	6
Chapter 2 Mentalism	19
Chapter 3 The Four Worlds & The Creative Process	24
Chapter 4 Theurgy & Transformation	31
Chapter 5 The Hermetic Qabalah	35
Chapter 6 The Ten Sephiroth	40
Chapter 7 The Master Pattern	51
Part II The Lesser Mysteries	59
Chapter 8 The Kingdom	60
Chapter 9 The Foundation	68
Chapter 10 The Divine Splendor	75
Chapter 11 The Victory	85
Part III The Greater Mysteries	93
Chapter 12 The Portal	94
Chapter 13 The One Ego	100
Chapter 14 The One Will	109
Chapter 15 The Master of Compassion	119
Part IV The Supreme Mysteries	125
Chapter 16 Across the Abyss	126
Chapter 17 The Qabalah & The Big Bang	132
Chapter 18 The Womb of Creation	134
Chapter 19 The Fountain of Light	144
Chapter 20 The Beginning	154

Part V The Serpent of Wisdom
Paths on the Tree of Life

Chapter 21 The Serpent of Wisdom	163
Chapter 22 The 32nd Path of Tav	169
Chapter 23 The 31st Path Letter Shin	177
Chapter 24 The 30th Path of Resh	181
Chapter 25 The 29th Path of Qoph	185
Chapter 26 The 28th Path of Tzaddi	191
Chapter 27 The 27th Path of Peh	196
Chapter 28 The 26th Path of Ayin	201
Chapter 29 The 25th Path of Samakh	206
Chapter 30 The 24th Path of Nun	213
Chapter 31 The 23rd Path of Mem	218
Chapter 32 The 22nd Path of Lamed	221
Chapter 33 The 21st Path of Kaph	229
Chapter 34 The 20th Path of Yod	234
Chapter 35 The 19th Path of Teth	240
Chapter 36 The 18th Path of Cheth	245
Chapter 37 The 17th Path of Zain	249
Chapter 38 The 16th Path of Vav	253
Chapter 39 The 15th Path of Heh	257
Chapter 40 The 14th Path of Daleth	263
Chapter 41 The 13th Path of Gimel	269
Chapter 42 The 12th Path of Beth	274
Chapter 43 The 11th Path of Aleph	279
Chapter 44 The Mystery of Theurgy	283
Chapter 45 The Pilgrim on The Path	286
Diagrams of the Tree of Life	289
The Pattern on the Trestleboard	293
Bibliography	294
Index	296

Table of Diagrams

The Hebrew Alphabet..	26
The Tree of Life...	41
Malkuth..	49
The Three Supernals..	53
Triad of the Higher Self..	55
Triad of the Personality..	55
Malkuth on the Tree...	56
The Components of Malkuth..	64
The Magical Image of Malkuth.....................................	67
The Magical Image of Yesod...	74
The Magical Image of Yod..	84
The Magical Image of Netzach.....................................	91
The Imbalance of Personality.......................................	97
The Magical Image of Tiphareth...................................	108
The Magical Image of Geburah....................................	118
The Magical Image of Chesed......................................	124
The Cube of Space...	141
The Magical Image of Binah...	143
Yod...	149
The Magical Image of Kether.......................................	160
The Serpent of Wisdom on the Tree of Life.................	162
Sulphur..	258
The Tree in the Four Worlds..	289
The Tree of Life & the Paths..	290
Planetary Attributions and the Zodiac.........................	291
The Tree in the Tree..	292

Acknowledgments

In every person's life he encounters people who are special and without whose influence he would not achieve his potential. These are his or her mentors. I have been especially blessed to have many who are my foundation. My spiritual mentors are, Paul Foster Case, Ann Davies, Eugene Emard, and Richard Talbot. My secular mentors are my father and mother, Lee and Artie Clark, my sister Margie and brothers Jimmy, John, and Sonny. My Masonic mentors are Ernie Morris and John Demille. My editors are Dee Morgan and Cindy Forbes. Any man who says he is self-made is either a fool or a liar. My thanks to all of these individuals.

Special Thanks to Alisha Jonreau for creating the Magical Images of the Sephiroth.

Finally I would like to acknowledge the inspiration of T.S. Elliot, who wrote:

"We shall not cease from exploration, and the end of our exploring will be to arrive where we started and know the place for the first time"

Dedications

This book is dedicated to my spiritual brother J.B. Morgan.

And also to my sons, Michael and Richard and my daughter, Kristen.

You have contributed much beauty and happiness to my life.

THE HERMETIC QABALAH

Introduction

To them I speak in parables. But unto you it is given to know the truth.

—Jesus the Nazarene

There has always existed a system of teaching that has its origin in the direct, personal experience of human beings dedicated to discovering the meaning of Life. These Adepts, or men and women of exceptional quality, have been labeled "the esoteric teachers." They, through the Ages, have passed on their wisdom by conveying detailed explanations of the meaning of their realizations. Throughout the centuries, these Adepts have codified and adopted the methods of this transmission for each succeeding generation, thus making it suitable for the aspirants of the day. This is for the present age of seekers the purpose of this work. These teachings did not originate with the author. He is merely the scribe. The source of this doctrine, the real author, is sometimes known as the "Inner School."

THE HERMETIC QABALAH

In the West, one of the greatest vehicles for this transmission is the Qabalistic Tree of Life. It is much more than a diagram. As W.E. Butler, the late, great teacher of the Western Mysteries once wrote:

> ...it is the result of many centuries of training and experience gathered into pictorial form, it is also an instrument through which certain energies and forces may be contacted by successive generations of students. [*Magic and the Qabalah*, p. 18]

The Tree is more than a manual. It embodies a system of training that instructs us to think in a specific way. The Tree is designed to train individuals in mental discipline so that they may develop a system of relational thinking. This system teaches the student to use the mind in a practical way, which will then enlighten his or her awareness, and enable the seeker to answer the ultimate questions concerning the nature of God, the Universe, and the soul of Man.

The Qabalah is thought to have been introduced into Hebrew theology just after the conclusion of the Babylonian captivity. At that time, the Scribes, who were tasked with civilizing the Israelite Nation following their return to the Holy Land, codified the Hebrew religious doctrines using the methods taught to them by the Babylonian wise men. Together, they integrated the scriptures, the secret teachings, and the consciousness training methods of the esoteric tradition.

This "enfolding" was modified and strengthened over the centuries by the contributions of the mystical traditions of the Egyptians, Chaldeans, and Greeks.

THE HERMETIC QABALAH

These teachings provided a system that trained the mind of the Initiate to be used so that it integrated its various levels and established direct contact with the dynamic forces of the Archetypes, and through them, to the creative power of God.

This goal is attained by regular and persistent meditation on the Tree of Life.

What exactly is the Qabalah? It is generally defined as the secret, mystical, magical, philosophical, and religious doctrines developed by ancient and medieval Jewish scholars as a key to the interpretation of the spiritual teachings of the scriptures. The Hermetic Qabalah is a term used to designate that core system as it has been enriched by neo-Platonic, Sufi, Hermetic and Christian mystical sources.

The word Qabalah means "tradition" and refers to the Esoteric Tradition. It comes from a Hebrew verb-root QBL, "Qebel" which means "to receive." Therefore, it carries the meaning of a received tradition.

As we have previously pointed out, while the ancient teachings were brought out of Egypt when the Hebrews emigrated from that land, it was codified, enriched, and given rebirth during the period following the release of the Hebrews from the Babylonian captivity.

It is believed that at this time the "Flame Alphabet" was introduced, as well as the systems of the Literal Qabalah (Gematria, Notariqon, and Temurah.)

THE HERMETIC QABALAH

The Flame Alphabet is important because with it, originated the systems of correspondence as well as the hieroglyphic nature of the figures. The alphabet could then be used as a series of objects or as the basis for meditational practices, etc.

THE HERMETIC QABALAH

PART I

General Considerations

THE HERMETIC QABALAH

Chapter 1

The Hermetic Principles

During the second half of the twentieth century, we see the emergence of a "new physics." This physics moves away from the mechanistic model of the universe prevalent in the nineteenth century, and moves closer to the metaphysical view of a conscious universe expounded by the Hermetic philosophers.

Will matter and mysticism meet?

It is exciting to see the points of agreement between the fundamentals of Hermeticism and the theories of Quantum Physics, more particularly, the holographic Theory of the Universe.

In this chapter we will explore the seven fundamental principles of the Hermetic School of Qabalah. For a more detailed examination, we refer you to the excellent book, *The Kybalion*, listed in the bibliography.

THE HERMETIC QABALAH

It will be seen how these ancient postulates seem to be supported by modern science—particularly physics.

Hermes Trismegistus

The "Corpus Hermeticum," gets its name from Trismegistus (Thrice-Great or Greatest of the great) Hermes. Traditionally, Hermes is known as the legendary Egyptian sage identified by the Greeks as the Egyptian god Thoth. However, there is evidence to suggest that the title, "Hermes" referred to a succession of sages who held an office similar to that of the Hierophant of the Eleusinian mysteries in Greece. The Thrice Greatest was thought to have been a contemporary of the patriarch Abraham. However, the Hermetic literature, as we have it, was most likely written at the time of the Common Era, either at the beginning of or just before.

Hermes was the reputed author of the Ritual of the Coming Forth by Day, which is better known as, *The Egyptian Book of the Dead*, which in reality is an initiation ritual.

Further, he is the supposed author of the famed Emerald Tablet. Legend says that this stone tablet was found by Alexander the Great in the tomb of Hermes in Egypt. It is quoted on the next page to give the reader an idea of the flavor of the writing and how it foreshadows certain modern scientific principles.

THE HERMETIC QABALAH

The Emerald Tablet of Hermes

Truth, without falsehood, certain and most true, that which is above is as that which is below, and that which is below is as that which is above, for to perform the miracles of the One Thing. From One do all things originate. By One are all mediated. All things have their birth from this One thing by adaptation.

Its Father is the Sun. Its Mother is the Moon. The Wind carries it in its belly. The Earth is its nurse. This is the Father of all perfection or consummation of the whole world. It is integrating if it be turned into earth.

Separate the earth from the fire, the subtle from the gross, suavely, and with great ingenuity. It ascends from earth to heaven and descends again to earth. Hence it gains or receives the greater and the lesser. So thou hast the glory of the whole world. Therefore let all obscurity vanish before thee.

This is the strong force of all forces, overcoming every subtle and penetrating every solid thing. Thus were the worlds created. Thus were all wonderful adaptations after this manner.

Therefore I am called Thrice Greatest Hermes and have the three components of the total philosophy of the world. I have completed what I have to tell concerning the Operation of the Sun.

THE HERMETIC QABALAH

The Seven Hermetic Principles

Like physics, the metaphysics of the Hermetic School has its own laws or principles. Whereas the laws of modern physics are built up by the observation of objective phenomena, the Hermetic principles use the instrument of the awakened, illumined consciousness of the Seer.

Here follows a summary of each of the Hermetic Principles. The quotes of the Seven Principles are taken from the book, *The Kybalion,* by Three Initiates. The commentary is the present author's. (See bibliography for further information of this classic reference work on Hermeticism.)

Mentalism

The Principle of Mentalism is so important and foundational that I have devoted a full chapter to its elucidation. Here, I will just say that it explains the mystery of creation both on the universal and personal level.

Correspondence

> "As above, so below; as below, so above."

This principle expresses the truth that nothing occurring in one segment of the Universe is isolated in effect from any other part.

> ...So Elohim created eth-ha-Adam (the Spirit of Humankind). In the image of the Elohim (the seven creative aspects of Deity) created They them. Male and Female created They them. [*Genesis* 1:27]

THE HERMETIC QABALAH

If the ALL is considered the greater world of the macrocosm, then Man is the microcosm. One is the reflection of the other. Or, as the Qabalah puts it, "Kether is in Malkuth and Malkuth is in Kether—but after another manner."

There are many planes or levels of expression that are unknown to us, but by applying the Principle of Correspondence we have a rule or guidepost that enables us to speculate on much that would otherwise remain unknowable. According to the law of correspondence, what holds true for one part of the Universe holds true throughout the whole. Every physical and tangible problem or pleasure has a mental and intangible correspondent. If we are able to identity these correspondences, we can often solve a problem by going to a higher level and gaining dominion over the factors of the situation. This means that when we are able to change our minds, or to change our feelings about something or someone (which is a higher level than the body), the body will reflect or project that kind of change. This change in the body will always be in conformity with the change in the mind.

When we examine the laws governing the growth of living things, we can learn something about the higher invisible spheres. For example, if we look at the laws of thermodynamics, we learn something about the laws of Man. And when we examine the laws of Man we will learn something about the nature of God.

THE HERMETIC QABALAH

Vibration

This principle may be expressed as "Nothing rests; everything moves; everything vibrates."

This same ancient principle has been postulated by "String or M-Theory" and is currently being examined in the field of 21st century physics. Atomic physicists have observed that all matter is in a constant state of vibration. The "solid" chair we sit on is mostly composed of space. The solid part of it is actually made up of rapidly vibrating atomic particles, orbiting around even more-rapidly vibrating nuclei.

The principle of vibration explains that the differences between distinct manifestations of matter, energy, mind and even spirit, result, to a great extent, from varying rates of vibration. From the "source," to the densest expression of matter, everything is formed from the same vibrational substance. The higher the vibration is, the higher its position on the scale.

Our entire universe is now described by physical scientists as energy in constant movement. "He who understands the Principle of Vibration has grasped the scepter of power," say the Ancients. [*The Kybalion*, p.147]

Polarity

>...Everything is dual; everything has poles; everything has its pairs of opposites; like and unlike are the same; opposites are identical in nature, but different in degree; extremes meet; all truths are but half-truths; all paradoxes may be reconciled...

THE HERMETIC QABALAH

Which of us has not asked of a swimming partner who has dived first into the water, "How is it?" And he answers, "The water's just fine. Come on in!" Only to find out that what was just fine, is in fact freezing!

At what point does cold become hot? If we look at a thermometer, there is no indication when hot becomes cold or cold becomes hot. These are just opposite aspects of a concept we normally refer to as temperature.

The same could be said for *all* opposites. At dawn, who can say when Darkness stops and Light begins? What is the difference between "big" and "little" or "love" and "hate?" The difference consists of varied degrees between the extremes of the phenomenon.

Seekers have been told that everything in Life is an interplay of opposites. Further, they have learned that their consciousness is the reconciling, controlling factor functioning through all of manifestation. The Adept, through the act of "Polarization," may change any vibration such as "hate" to its opposite, "love." Here is the secret of mental alchemy and one of the explanations of the mysteries of the Crucifixion.

It is a fact that every manifestation on the material plane changes or affects everything else. If *all* was the same, then "no-*thing*" would matter. Would it? This is an infinite truth verifiable by basic reasoning. If there were no differences or distinctions in the world, there could be no materialization of any thought or thing.

THE HERMETIC QABALAH

Of course, the ultimate solution is to learn to live from that realm of absolute spirit, the realm of pure-mindedness. Here there is, as Charles Fillmore says, "no duality, no swinging back and forth from pole to pole." But, in that serene mind of the absoluteness of God, there is no materiality either.

Every stick has two ends. There is no way that we can have a pencil without two ends, no matter how close together they are. We may think that if we put the ends of the pencil closer and closer together that we can overcome the problem of having opposite ends. So we chop repeatedly, until there is nothing left materially! There must be pairs of opposites to define the range of manifestation. Without varying degrees between the extremes of polarity, materiality and visibility become nonexistent.

Rhythm

> ...Everything flows, out and in; everything has its tides; all things rise and fall; The pendulum-swing manifests in everything; the measure of the swing to the right is the measure of the swing to the left; rhythm compensates...

We are told that all things move in tides. The Bible says: "To everything there is a season and a time to every purpose under the heavens..." [*Ecclesiastes* 3:1] Traditionally, the year is divided in accordance with the four solar tides. The year begins with the tide of Planning, the period from the Autumnal Equinox to the Winter Solstice. The Tide of Introspection and Testing runs from the Winter Solstice to the Vernal Equinox. From the Vernal Equinox to the Summer Solstice we have the Tide of Planting. Finally, the Tide of Harvest occurs from the Summer Solstice to the Autumnal Equinox. Then the annual cycle repeats. This is but one of the cycles of which humanity has intuitive knowledge, and by which they plan their tasks. The true seeker learns how to apply these principles, rather than being ruled by them.

Humanity, in general, reacts from one extreme to another. An Adept rests himself at the point which he desires to rest, and then neutralizes the rhythmic swing of the pendulum, which would otherwise carry him to the opposite extreme. These Adepts (illuminated persons) have discovered what has been called the Principle of Neutralization. This principle works along with the Law of Inner Causation which states that each of us creates our universe from *within* through our habitual images and thoughts. Persons who are spiritually awakened withdraw to the higher or *inner* plane of causation. By fixing his or her consciousness on the outcome desired at this level, they rise above the undesired effect, and let it pass by. In so doing, they *neutralize* the counter-swing. Thus, by refusing to participate in the swing of mass-consciousness, they emerge as the master.

We can readily tabulate a number of different rhythms. These are observable in our physical universe. For example, the rhythm of sunrise and sunset, the rhythm of the tides of the ocean, the rhythm of the seasons, moving from one season to another occurs every year.

THE HERMETIC QABALAH

Yet, each season comes with its own distinctive flavor for that particular year. There is rhythm, sameness and continuity, but always with the touch and the color of variety.

We see rhythm not only in the physical universe, but in the history of humanity. There, we find a rhythmic cycle of reoccurrence.

There are also inner personal psychological rhythms which we may have sensed in ourselves and others. Sometimes, it's easier to objectively observe our companions than it is to observe ourselves. The awareness of rhythm is an objective study of the subjective world.

There are always peaks and valleys of emotional sensitivity. On a given day, constructive words of criticism may roll off our backs without a thought, but if the same words are uttered at a time when our sensitivity is more acute, *war* follows. There are also peaks and valleys in creative conception. Sometimes one can be creative with greater ease, greater originality, and greater inspiration than at other times.

There is an inner psychological cycle of dependence and independence. There are times when we need the support of something or somebody. Other times we have an equal need to assert greater independence. Reactions become more manageable when we have learned to manage ourselves.

THE HERMETIC QABALAH

Cause and Effect

> ...Every Cause has its Effect; every Effect has its Cause; everything happens according to Law; Chance is but a name for Law not recognized; there are many planes of causation, but nothing escapes the Law...

We cannot avoid the Principle of Cause and Effect, but we can choose to become one of the "Causers" rather than an "Effect." We should use this principle instead of it using us. Through desire, we ourselves may become vehicles for the Cosmic Administration and thus develop into conscious "co-creators."

This principle, expounded by Hermes thousands of years ago, is the basis of all modern scientific thought. The very word Universe implies this principle as does the word Cosmos.

This principle helps to show us in exactly what condition we are. As we consider the Law of Cause and Effect, we realize that every effect in our lives at this present moment was caused. There are no accidents. We had something to do with those causes. This helps us to understand why things are as they are. But to simply look in the mirror and observe, "My life looks like a mess," is no remedy. We must become the cause of our redemption.

Gender

> ...Gender is in everything; everything has its masculine and feminine principles; Gender manifests on all planes...

THE HERMETIC QABALAH

Electrons with a negative charge dance about protons carrying a positive charge. From the level of the atom to that of the galaxy and beyond, the Law of Gender operates.

In the Qabalah, the interplay of gender is symbolized by the relationship of the second and third Sephiroth of the Tree of Life, called Chokmah (Wisdom) and Binah (Understanding). The masculine projective energy represented by Chokmah is channeled to the feminine. The channel or path that is the vehicle for this interchange is assigned to the ideas of Love and Desire.

This principle explains that in every expression we will find both masculine and feminine characteristics. Modern psychology rediscovered the truth that, whatever physical vehicle we are expressing through in a particular incarnation, we have components of both the feminine and the masculine.

The power to beget or to produce or to provide a line of succession is manifest in animal and human organisms as sex. However, it is much more inclusive than this. From the tiniest unit of matter there is a coming together of positive charge and negative charge, masculine and feminine. Without this coming together nothing is created. Without this movement and exchange of distinctive qualities (which we symbolically describe as masculine and feminine), there is no spark or life.

When we are at a stage in our life where we feel nothing is happening, it is because the inner principles that correspond to the feminine-masculine are mismatched

THE HERMETIC QABALAH

or unmatched. Hence, as in the physical universe there can be only a flow of power through the interaction of positive and negative charges, so in our consciousness there can only be this flow of power when there is an interaction of positive and negative—the positive and negative aspects of our being. Both have a part to play.

In the next chapter we will have a closer look at the foundational Principle of Mentalism.

THE HERMETIC QABALAH

Chapter 2

Mentalism

An understanding of the *Otz Chaim* or Tree of Life is fundamental to an understanding of the Hermetic Qabalah. Not only is it a master diagram for correlating the massive amount of ideas, symbols, and concepts of the mystical system, it is a powerful tool for training the consciousness in relational or non-linear thinking.

Theurgy is a word that is usually translated as "God-working," but it will probably be easier to understand if we take it to mean creating or working in the same manner as the Divine.

The concept is explained by the Hermetic Principle of Mentalism:

"The All is Mind; The Universe is Mental."

This principle postulates that the substantial reality underlying all the outward manifestations and appearances of the material universe proceeded from

THE HERMETIC QABALAH

the thought processes of the Universal Mind, comparable to the consciousness of Man. But, whereas the human mind is finite in scope, that of the "ALL" is infinite.

As the authors of *The Kybalion* express it:

> ...An understanding of this great hermetic principle of Mentalism enables the individual to readily grasp the laws of the mental universe and to apply the same to his well-being and advancement. [*The Kybalion*, p. 27]

Further, when considering the question of the mental nature of the universe and the creative process, they write:

> ...What is the Universe? We have seen that there can be nothing outside of the ALL. Then, is the Universe the ALL? No, this cannot be, because the Universe seems to be made up of MANY, and is constantly changing...Then if the Universe is not the ALL, then it must be nothing—such is the evitable conclusion of the mind at first thought. But this will not satisfy the question, for we are sensible of the existence of this universe. Then, if the Universe is neither the ALL, nor Nothing, what can it be? [ibid, p. 66].

The authors then provide a theory of the nature of creation that is not only essential for understanding the Hermetic Qabalah but also of comprehending the entire rationale of the practice of initiation and the Mysteries:

THE HERMETIC QABALAH

>...If the Universe exists at all, or seems to exist, it must proceed in some way from the ALL—it must be a creation of the ALL. And as something can never come from nothing, from what could the ALL have created it? Some philosophers have answered this question by saying that the ALL created the Universe from ITSELF—that is, from the being and substance of the ALL. But this will not do, for the ALL cannot be subtracted from nor divided...and then again if this be so, would not each particle in the Universe be aware of its being the ALL?—The ALL could not lose its knowledge of itself, nor actively BECOME an atom, or blind force, or lowly living thing. Some men, indeed, realizing that the ALL, is indeed ALL and also recognizing that they, the men, existed, have jumped to the conclusion that they and the ALL were identical and have filled the air with shouts of "I AM GOD," to the amusement of the multitude and the sorrow of sages... [ibid, p. 66].

This problem of "from what is the Universe created?" is a problem that has vexed philosophers and religions throughout the ages. *The Kybalion* solves this question by utilizing the Hermetic Principle of Correspondence. This maxim states "As Above, So Below," and is taken from the *Emerald Tablet of Hermes*. Basically this principle states that the dynamics of cosmic forces can be explained by examining those on our own plane of expression.

>...On his own plane of being, how does Man create? Well, first, he may create by making

THE HERMETIC QABALAH

> something out of outside materials. But this will not do, for there are no materials outside of the ALL with which it may create. Well, then, secondly, Man creates or reproduces his kind by the process of begetting, which is self-multiplication accomplished by transferring a portion of this substance in the offspring. But this will not do, because the ALL cannot transfer or subtract a portion of itself nor can it reproduce or multiply itself. In the first place there would be a taking away and in the second case a multiplication or addition to the ALL, both thoughts being an absurdity.
>
> Is there a third way in which Man creates? Yes, there is—he CREATES MENTALLY! And in so doing, he uses no outside materials nor does he reproduce himself and yet his Spirit pervades the Mental Creation [ibid, p. 68]

Hermetic doctrine thus postulates that the ALL created the Universe in a manner akin to the process whereby Man creates mental images. In fact, when we examine the description of creation myths as reported by the illuminated sages of the past, we find them in complete agreement with this concept. The ALL constantly creates and sustains the Universe mentally. Everything that we see related to the manifested universe, ourselves included, exists as a construct of consciousness within the imagination of God.

> ...The ALL can create in no other way except mentally, without either using material (and there is none to use), or else reproducing

THE HERMETIC QABALAH

itself (which is also impossible). There is no escape from this conclusion of the Reason, which, as we have said, agrees with the highest teachings of the Illumined. [ibid, p. 69]

There is one basic difference. While the imaginative creations of humanity are finite, that of the ALL is the creation of an infinite consciousness.

...The Universe and all it contains is a mental creation of the ALL. [ibid, p. 70]

THE HERMETIC QABALAH

Chapter 3

The Four Worlds and the Creative Process

The ancient Qabalists described the Universe as having four modes of reality. These four expressions have now been mirrored in the works of depth psychologists, especially in the writings of the late Carl Gustav Jung, the founder of the school of Analytic Psychology. The Qabalists explained how the Creator of the Universe "imaged" the cosmos into manifestation. They asserted that despite appearances to the contrary, the creative process always starts in the realm of consciousness and proceeds, step-by-step towards the world of appearances, conditions and events.

This process may be summed up by the Law of Inner Causation, which states that:

> "Every clear, emotionally charged creative image will tend to manifest itself as an actual condition or event."

In fact, initiates are taught that never in the realm of outside appearances will be found anything that causes us to do, think, feel or be anything. It is our reaction to these outside stimuli that determines our reality. They are simply our "magic mirrors" that reveal to us the inner health or disease of our creative process.

THE HERMETIC QABALAH

The truth is we co-create with the Divine our experience of reality moment-to-moment based on the mental images we habitually hold and choose to energize. This is verifiable to any clear thinking individual. Pick any event you are experiencing and follow the events, decisions, choices—the chain of causation—and it will be seen that the causes of that sequence were principally mental.

By referencing the Principle of Correspondence, Initiates of the Qabalah reasoned that if this was true for humans, then it would remain true on the higher planes. Thus Qabalists postulate that there are four planes of consciousness. They call them "Olahms" or worlds.

Atziluth

The first of these is called Atziluth, which is roughly translated as "Primal." Some writers have called this the "Divine" world, but this tends to lead to the idea that God is only present at the Atziluthic level which is incorrect. Others call it the realm of the Archetypes. This is also incorrect and is probably based upon S.L. MacGregor-Mather's unfortunate choice of terms in his introduction to his translation of Knorr von Rosenroth's *Kabbalah Denudata* (*Kabbalah Unveiled*). As we shall see, Archetypes come into play in the second world, not Atziluth.

What then is the mode of Atziluth? This is the mode of pure energy, before any restriction or definition. Here is infinite potential, the white light containing all the colors of the spectrum. Here, indeed is Bohu (BHU), the

THE HERMETIC QABALAH

Hebrew word for "the Void." It is from this void that all emerges.

Bohu, by Gematria, the Literal Qabalah numbering system, equals thirteen.

In Gematria, each letter of the Hebrew alphabet is also a number. (This is literally true, for ancient Hebrew had no separate number symbols. They used the letters to represent numbers).

Hebrew	Letter	Number	Hebrew	Letter	Number
א	Aleph, A	1	ל	Lamed, L	30
ב	Beth, B(V)	2	מ	Mem, M	40
ג	Gimel, G	3	נ	Nun, N	50
ד	Daleth, D	4	ס	Samekh, S	60
ה	Heh, H	5	ע	Ayin, O (Ag, Ng)	70
ו	Vav, V(U)	6	פ	Peh, P (f)	80
ז	Zain, Z	7	צ	Tzaddi, Tz	90
ח	Cheth, Ch	8	ק	Qoph, Q	100
ט	Teth, T	9	ר	Resh, R	200
י	Yod, I (Y,J)	10	ש	Shin, Sh (S)	300
כ	Kaph, K	20	ת	Tav, Th (T)	400

Diagram #1   The Hebrew Alphabet

THE HERMETIC QABALAH

There are also five "final forms" of letters, or special forms, that are used when a letter comes at the end of the word. These are generally are not used in Gematria:

Kaph final = 500;   Mem final = 600;   Nun final = 700;   Ayin final = 800;   Peh final = 900.

Bohu therefore adds as follows:

B = 2

H = 5

U = <u>6</u>

    13

This is especially significant in our discussion of Atziluth because thirteen is also the number of Echud (AChD 1+8+4) "Unity" and Ahevah (AHBH 1+5+2+5) "Love."

A meditative phrase used to describe this level might read, "Atziluth represents the level at which God is acting as the great void that produces oneness and love."

The mode of consciousness at Atziluth is "I." Just "I," no differentiation, no restriction, there is just identity. It is pure Divine energy.

Briah

Briah is the Hebrew name for the World of Creation. Here, the white light of Atziluth is broken up by the prism of the archetypes (the universal primal forms)

THE HERMETIC QABALAH

into the many colors. There are nine basic Qabalistic archetypes. Note that there are also nine major gods, goddesses or archangels of most of the great religions of the classical period. Also this is probably the reason for the ten Sephiroth (or major categories) of the Tree of Life. The tenth Sephirah, Malkuth is assigned to Earth as the field of expression of the archetypes.

In Briah, the energy of the ONE expresses itself as consciousness. This is what is termed the "I Am" expressing as essential reality. The "I" of Atziluth has now acquired attributes. These are expressed, for example, as Venus, Goddess of Love; Mars, God of War, etc.

Perhaps this is easier to illustrate using the Hebrew system of archangels. Archangelic names are not really names at all, but rather, titles describing function and archetypes. For example, "Raphael" means "Healing of God," while "Auriel" means "Light of God," etc.

The world of Briah is usually what is referred to as the World of Spirit, although this is an arbitrary distinction. Mind and Matter are simply manifestations of spirit that falls within certain vibratory limits. Briah is not usually experienced except in rare moments of mystical ecstatic visionary states.

Yetzirah

The next world is called Yetzirah which means "formation." It is the level of Mythic Reality and is the realm of the imagination. Here the energy expresses itself through symbols and images. The mode of

THE HERMETIC QABALAH

consciousness expressing here has been labeled by Dr. Jean Huston as, "This is We." This is appropriate because in Yetzirah the emphasis is on unity. We find this expressed as the Astral Plane, the Collective Unconsciousness, and the Akashic Records.

Mythic Reality is a term used to designate the power of symbol, ritual, and legend. At this level, we find the images of legendary figures, both good and bad. Here is Santa Claus, the Wizard of Oz, Dumbledore as well as the Grinch, the Wicked Witch, and Voldemort.

Special attention should be paid to the characters of myths and also the symbols of tradition, be they astrological, alchemical, or the sacred alphabets. At this level of consciousness they are connected to great reservoirs of conscious energy that may be tapped and directed by the trained imagination.

Assiah

Assiah is the world of manifest reality. Note "manifest" is just one kind of reality—not the only kind, as asserted by the Materialist. However, we also don't go to the other extreme and proclaim, "All is Maya, and all is illusion." Often what is illusionary is our interpretation of the manifest reality. The physical world is the arena of appearances, conditions, and events. These are the effects of the creation process, not the cause. We ignore them at our peril. For these effects act as our measuring stick or mirror, that we may observe the outcomes of our creative acts of mind and body. The cause is within.

THE HERMETIC QABALAH

Here, the Divine energy acts through form and vibration. True, sometimes the form might not be perceptible to our senses, but even these interact with us through the vibratory patterns they possess.

An example of the how the Four Worlds operate in relation to each other could be illustrated, for instance, with the example of a chair.

At Atziluth, we find Divine Potential, all of the energy we need for our creation. At Briah, we have the archetypal idea of sitting. Yetzirah provides us with the many images and "types" of chairs. We have sofas, captain chairs, thrones, etc. We select one most suited to our needs, say a recliner or easy chair and in Assiah, we either build it or buy it. Then, through this act of creation, we may enjoy the act of sitting.

In the next chapter we will look at how masters use this process to achieve their full potential.

THE HERMETIC QABALAH

Chapter 4

Theurgy & Spiritual Transformation

Theurgy or "High Magic" literally translates as "God Working." Its history is venerable indeed and is easily traced back to the most ancient civilizations of India, Tibet, China, Chaldea, and Egypt. The Hebrew Commandment prohibiting worship of "graven images" probably has its source in an abuse or perversion of the practice of Theurgy. In these malpractices, the spiritual force generated by a theurgical operation would focus on an idol, even to the extent of embodying in the graven image an elemental of the lower sort. These statues would then be the object of worship. This displacement would then be promoted by an unethical priesthood so that they could manipulate the populace.

In true Theurgy, the focus of the spiritual power is the theurgist him or herself. The object of this practice is the transformation of the individual to achieve his or her full, divine potential.

THE HERMETIC QABALAH

In the last chapter we examined the critical role Archetypes play in the creative process. These powerful "lenses" focus a specific aspect of the divine consciousness. This archetype then becomes the original matrix that is linked to the symbols in Yetzirah which, in turn, finally become embodied in some manifested form in Assiah.

The ancient adepts knew that every archetype in the macrocosm had a direct correlation in the microcosm or individual consciousness of Man. In other words, the consciousness of man mirrors the consciousness of the Cosmic. Once again we have, "As above, so below."

Freemasonry uses the symbol of the "rough ashlar" or a stone taken fresh from the quarry in its rough, unsquared state as a symbol for the consciousness of natural man. This natural man or rough ashlar is a product of the natural evolutionary process. But, Man is destined for a greater, more sublime purpose—to become a conscious vehicle of the cosmic creative process.

How is this achieved? Well, Nature itself cannot achieve it because, as the ancient alchemists say, "Nature unaided always fails." Man alone cannot achieve this either, for, as the Psalmist tell us, "Unless the Lord builds the house, they labor in vain who build it." [*Psalms* 127:1] What is required is the establishment of a co-creatorship; a partnership of the Divine with the Human. This is what Theurgy achieves. Through Theurgy the rough stone is smoothed and shaped, fitted for the Builder's use.

THE HERMETIC QABALAH

Working with the pattern and system of the Tree of Life, each component of our personality consciousness is selectively awakened and activated. This is done in a balanced sequence so that one part or function is not emphasized at the expense of another. The outer consciousness is followed by that of the inner; the intellect by the emotions, until a dynamic equilibrium is established producing a personality capable of expressing the high tensioned energy of the Holy Guardian Angel within.

One of the archetypes is selected to be used as a targeted intention. The Qabalist then meditates on the selected focus using relational thinking expressed through the various images, symbols, designations, and attributions he has been trained to associate with the selected form.

In this manner, a symbolic bridge, or chain of images, is formed in the consciousness of the Theurgist. This then acts as a linking mechanism capable of transmitting the transformative energy of the archetype from the level of Briah across the world of Yetzirah to stimulate the individual and find expression in the world of time and space that is, the Qabalistic world of Assiah.

This activation sets in motion a reaction in the manifest world that presents to the aspirant various events, relationships, and challenges that may be used to refine, balance and define a transformative level of consciousness.

THE HERMETIC QABALAH

In this way, the Qabalist may arrive at a point where he can in reality assert, as the Pattern on the Trestleboard states: "The Kingdom of Spirit is embodied in my flesh."

For the complete Pattern on the Trestleboard please refer to the Appendix.

THE HERMETIC QABALAH

Chapter 5

The Hermetic Qabalah

Many consider the Qabalah to be a distinctly Jewish phenomenon. It is true that the term historically refers to a mystical system developed by medieval Jewish scholars as a key to the interpretation of the spiritual teachings of their scriptures. However, as explained in the introduction, it is much more than that. This system has been enriched by Neo-Platonist, Sufi, and Christian mystical sources. It is for this reason that we have chosen the term "Hermetic Qabalah" to differentiate it from the more orthodox, purely Jewish version.

In Hebrew, the word Qabalah (QBLH) means "tradition." It is derived from the root Qebel (QBL) which means "to receive" or "the reception" and carried the connotation of an oral tradition, transmitted from mouth to ear. When translated into English, it is sometimes spelled Kabbalah, Cabala, or Qabalah,

THE HERMETIC QABALAH

depending upon the academic field and school of training of the writer.

There is an allegorical tradition that says God taught the Qabalah to the angels in Paradise. Ratziel, the Archangel of Wisdom, passed this teaching along to humanity after the fall, so that we might use it to return to a state of grace.

Historically, the Qabalah is based on several ancient sources. Egypt was one of them, and this is one of the meanings behind the Biblical reference to Moses and Aaron being versed in the crafts of the temples.

Babylon was another important source. When the Hebrews were exiled into Babylon, the intelligencia mingled with the wise of their captors and were introduced into their mysteries. When they were returned to Palestine, a number of Scribes were tasked with civilizing the resident population and establishing a culture. It was probably at this time that the Torah was codified from other ancient, traditional texts. For certain, this is when the ancient mystical tradition was introduced into the scriptures, such as Gematria and the Flame alphabet, with its built-in code of meditational correspondences. This tradition later became the Qabalah.

A proto-qabalah was taught and practiced at the "School of the Prophets" and later in the Essene and Nazarean communities.

After the destruction of the second temple in Jerusalem by the Romans, Merkabah or Chariot mysticism,

THE HERMETIC QABALAH

comprising elaborate elements of Jewish Mysticism spread with the Diaspora of the Jews.

The Hermetic Qabalah with its varied antecedents probably originated in Alexandria, Egypt. Schools were also established in Fez, Morocco, and the South of Spain.

When the Jews were expelled from Spain by Ferdinand and Isabella, they carried their teachings throughout Europe.

Francis Yates, in her seminal work, *The Occult Philosophy in the Elizabethan Age*, gives an excellent historical review of how the ancient wisdom carried by these wandering refugees became one of the major factors initiating the European Renaissance.

Two great centers of learning were established as a result of this dispersion. One was in Florence under the protection of Cosmo de Medici, which gave birth to the Christian Cabala. Additionally, it was here that the Corpus Hermeticum or body of Hermetic writings was first translated into Latin.

The second center was located in Safed in Galilee. This center produced the great Kabalists Moses Cordavero and Isaac Luria.

The combination of these varied influences became the foundation of the Hermetic Qabalah. This mighty current of the Hermetic Qabalah became the mainstream of the Western Mystery Tradition and as

THE HERMETIC QABALAH

historians are only now beginning to realize, profoundly influenced the course of Western History.

The Classic Texts

Original Qabalistic texts are very difficult to trace. Such writings were kept secret by those who used them, and they were destroyed as heretical if discovered by the secular and ecclesiastic authorities. It is believed that the oldest extant written classic of the Qabalah is the *Sepher Yetzirah* or Book of Formation. This work, together with the *Thirty-two Paths of Wisdom*, deals with the symbolism of creation, of numbers, and of letters. It is thought to have been compiled by Rabbi Akiba, circa 120 A.D., from older writings.

The Bahir or *Book of Illumination* is attributed to Rabbi Nehunia ben ha-Kana. This work made its appearance during the first or second century and, "...explores the methodology of the ancient Kabbalists, stressing the meditative techniques that were essential to their discipline..." [Aryeh Kaplan, *"The Bahir"*].

Perhaps the best known Qabalistic classic is *The Zohar* or the *Book of Splendor*. This work, or rather collection of works, is attributed to the Qabalistic Saint, Rabbi Simeon ben Jochai; although it is doubtful the entire work is by any one hand. Rabbi Jochai, a disciple of Akiba, was sentenced to death by Lucius Verus, the co-regent of Emperor Marcus Aurelius Antonius. The Rabbi had presumably drawn the wrath of the ruler for espousing political heresies and was forced to flee with his son into the wilderness where they hid in a cave for twelve years. During this period of extreme hardship,

THE HERMETIC QABALAH

as the legend is told, he received, through inspiration, *The Zohar*. The book remained unpublished until the 14th century when it was made public by Moses ben Shem Tob de Leon. Its first Latin translation was published at Frankfort in 1677 by Knorr von Rosenroth as the *Kabbalah Denudata*. This was, in turn, made available in English by S.L. MacGregor Mathers as *The Kabbalah Unveiled*.

Other Qabalistic classics include: *The Aesh Mezareph*, or *The Book of the Purifying Fire*, a Qabalistic-Alchemical treatise and *The Sepher Ratziel*, a Qabalistic-Magical work. Two classics of the Christian Cabala are Marsillo Ficino's *The Book of Life*, and Johann Reuchlin's *De Arte Cabalistica*. The Safedic Jewish Kabbalah is aptly represented by Isaac Luria's *Ten Luminous Emanations*, and Abulatia's *Path of the Names*.

Excellent modern Qabalistic classics are represented by Paul Foster Case's *The Book of Tokens*, Dion Fortune's *The Mystical Qabalah*, and the works of Aryeh Kaplan.

Every serious student of the Qabalah should eventually aspire to read many of these books. Most are currently available. It should be remembered that many works of the "Receptive Tradition" are often written not to inform (that is to deliver facts), but rather to train the mind in the process by which one becomes receptive to the instruction of one's own Inner Teacher.

THE HERMETIC QABALAH

Chapter 6

The Ten Sephiroth

The images held in Yetzirah determine the physical manifestations in our daily lives. If we desire change, we must first change the patterns on which these manifestations are based. The more perfectly these inner patterns mirror universal truth, the more aligned we will become with the forces of the cosmos and the more our lives will be filled with joy, peace, and true success.

Most people have no overall plan or only a fragmented one at best. So almost any organized system would be an improvement. There are many groups offering guidelines for living. Qabalists have the advantage of being able to adopt the pattern actually used by Illuminated Adepts to perfect their own lives.

The Tree of Life (see diagram #2) is called the Master Pattern. It is a circuit diagram of the flow of forces from the inner, causative levels to outer, personal, physical levels.

THE HERMETIC QABALAH

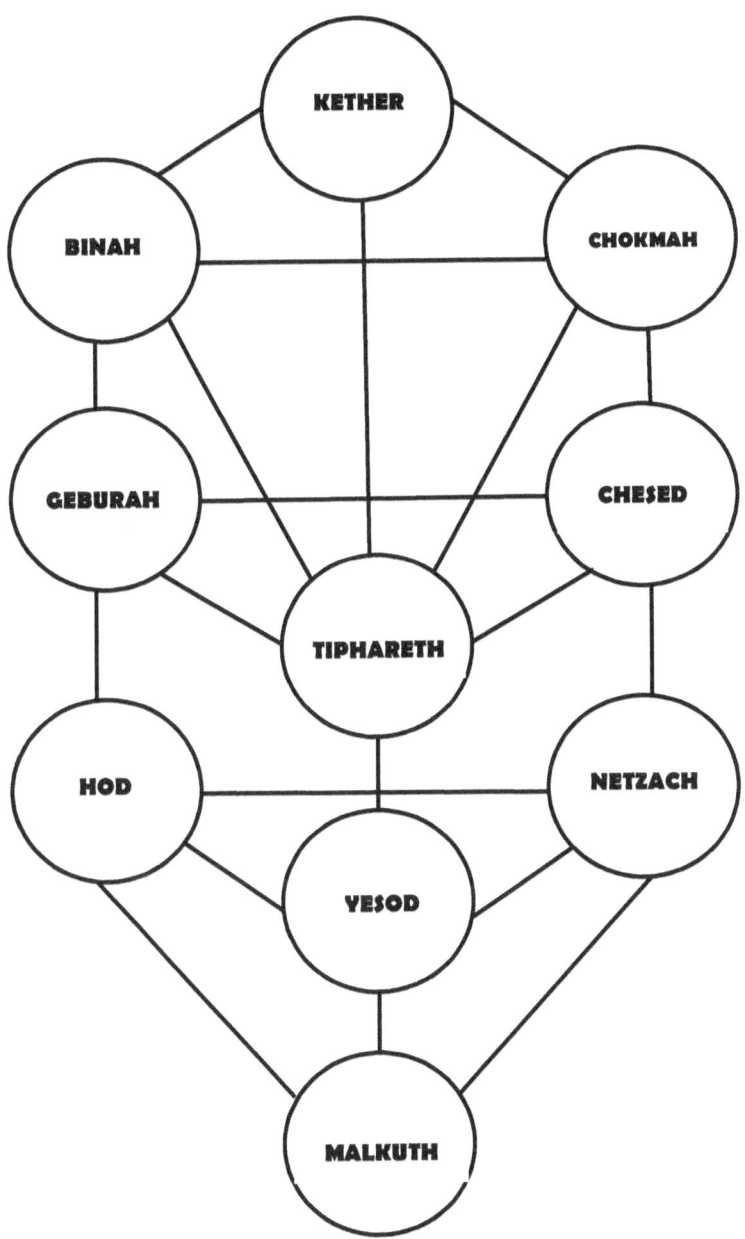

Diagram #2   The Tree of Life

THE HERMETIC QABALAH

It is a code of conduct. It shows the relationships of aspects of your consciousness to all other major esoteric symbol systems. Like a Rosetta Stone of consciousness, it helps to decode the truth behind many systems of inner teachings. No man can claim to know all about the Tree. The Tree of Life can become a meditational mandala, blueprint, and study assignment in different forms for a lifetime.

Let us examine the major components of the Tree of Life. The aspects listed here are only a brief introduction, but will provide a framework onto which you can build. The goal of our study is not the empty mental exercise of trying to compile the longest list of attributions. The goal is to become the Tree.

Kether

The word Kether means "the Crown." It is the first outpouring of the Limitless Light, the Primal Will, the Ancient of Days, and the Cosmic Unity. In the Macrocosm, it is the Godhead, source of all existence. In the Microcosm, it symbolizes the divine spark which unites us with the Ultimate Deity, the Great Unmanifest which can neither be named nor defined. It is also called "The Beginning of the Whirlings." Kether is the root of the Tree of Life.

Chokmah

Chokmah is the Hebrew word for Wisdom. It symbolizes the Supernal Father, the seed. While Kether is considered the first aspect of positive existence and is symbolized by a point, the simplest geometrical concept, Chokmah is the next stage—direction. Direction

THE HERMETIC QABALAH

indicates movement with purpose. Its symbol is the line. It represents absolute potential—energy not yet restricted by form: explosive, all powerful, unbridled expansion. Chokmah is the head of the Masculine Pillar of force. Astrologically it corresponds to the Zodiac.

Binah

Binah means Understanding. This is representative of the Divine Mother, the Cosmic Womb, and the Great Sea. The third Sephirah is at the head of the feminine and form side of the Tree. As the projective power of the line of Chokmah starts to move, the magnetic energy of Binah attracts and shapes the projection into a curve—creating the structure of time and space. This limiting aspect of Binah is seen again in this correspondence with time through its attribution to Saturn, Father Time. In the Microcosm, Binah is the seat of the Neshamah or Divine Soul, the Holy Spirit of Christian theology. She is the source of intuition. She confines, directs and concentrates the force of Chokmah and is therefore the Mother of all creation.

Chesed

Chesed means Mercy and is aligned with compassion, anabolism or the force that builds up, and the faculty of memory.

This Sephirah is the highest of the Triangle of Individuality. To it is attributed the planet Jupiter. Jupiter was the king of the Greek pantheon, and thus it is appropriate that the magical image of Chesed is that of a wise and just king, a benevolent ruler.

THE HERMETIC QABALAH

This Just King administers the kingdom according to the laws of the Cosmos. Chesed is also the level assigned to the Chasidim or the Lords of Compassion. Microcosmically, Chesed is attributed to Memory, not the personal memory, but rather the universal memory of creation. At the level of awakening symbolized by Chesed, Man "remembers" who is God, what is the Universe, why he was created and the purpose of his existence. True compassion is always in balance with a firm Justice which is represented by the next Sephirah, Geburah.

Geburah

Geburah or Severity is also called Pachad (Fear) and Din (Justice). These titles describe the three ways Man usually reacts to God's power. Primitive Man views God with awe or fear. He attempts to propitiate the forces he fears in hopes they will favor him. The more "advanced" Man views the universe as a huge inflexible, severe mechanism, governed by cold unresponsive forces that will smash any person unlucky enough to run afoul of their inexorable rule. This viewpoint is what is termed Materialism, a belief which leads to placing all one's energy into physical acquisitions based on the assumption that the physical is all there is. Its fault lies in its foundation, a partial picture of the true universe. It views the outer world of effects as the total reality and remains ignorant of the inner world of cause. Contrary to Materialism's goals, the person who acquires the most possessions is not always the winner.

To the few in every generation there comes a vision of the higher. To those the manifested universe is the

THE HERMETIC QABALAH

luminous image of its Creator and they see that all laws are manifestations of conscious principles of Universal Justice and Love.

Geburah corresponds to Mars, action, will, law, and to catabolism (the breaking down of the old so that the new can be built). In Man, the Geburian aspect manifests as the power of Volition or Will. We have no need to develop will-power. True Will is a Cosmic power, not a personal characteristic and is exhaustlessly available to all. In early and perhaps in intermediate stages of the training of the Hermetic Qabalist, it does appear that the discipline required is a function of our will-power, but when we accept the reality that our Will is an aspect of the Universal, when we realize that we "have no will save to do the Will of He who sent me," [*John* 6:38] the power of the Universe shall flow through us. Adepts all report that once we reach the stage where we can truly see, we will know that no matter how it appears at the time, our progress on the Path has not been a result of our personal striving from below, but rather originates in the gentle pull of a benevolent hand from above.

Tiphareth

Tiphareth (sometimes spelled Tifareth) means Beauty. It is assigned to the Ego, Christ, the Messiah, the Sacrificed God, and the Priest King. Macrocosmically, Tiphareth also corresponds to the Sun; the center of consciousness that makes all life in our solar system possible. Microcosmically, it refers to the Individuality, the real Self that is an extension of the Solar Logos. It is this aspect of consciousness that reincarnates again

THE HERMETIC QABALAH

and again until the destiny of perfection is achieved and identity with the Logoidal Consciousness is complete. It is important to make it clear that attainment of this goal does not mean a loss of identity, as some mistakenly interpret the Eastern teaching of Nirvana. On the contrary, we are told by those who have gone before that the only loss is that the false self of the ego is realized for what it is—a very small part of the whole. With this realization we receive direct knowledge and awareness of the very uniqueness and scope of the True Self.

Netzach

Netzach means Victory. It corresponds to the Green Ray of Nature and Power, to Venus, and the ancient element of fire. Netzach is the highest Sephirah of the Personality Triad and is the seat of the emotions and the Desire Force. According to the alchemists this force must be purified and turned "white." There is a mistaken idea among some spiritual aspirants that they must achieve a state of "desirelessness." The excellent book, *Light on the Path* by Mabel Collins, even states that the Disciple must, "kill out desire." But careful reading further clarifies the goal. What must, in reality, be killed out are the misinterpretations of this force. No desire originates at the personality level. All desires are really Divine in origin. No matter how distorted, how selfish, how base they manifest to our perception, they are all rooted in the One Self's longing to be one with Its creation.

The desire is pure. Our methods for fulfilling it, however, often need to be re-examined and restructured.

THE HERMETIC QABALAH

Our selfish interpretations may need to be sacrificed until the holiness of this force is realized.

Without Desire we would have no motivation and would become aspirationally dead. We would become like a boat in the ocean without oars or sail or motor. With no means of propulsion we would simply drift with the currents and be at the mercy of the storms. The Sages tell us to "Inflame yourself with prayer!" A fiery emotion is a prerequisite for spiritual advancement.

Hod

The eighth Sephirah is called Hod, which is Hebrew for Splendor. It corresponds to Mercury and the Ray of Wisdom. The eighth Sephirah is the compliment of the seventh. While Netzach concerns the emotions of our personality, Hod is the sphere of thoughts or the intellect. It is also attributed to the ancient element of Water. Let us examine this water and see why it was chosen to represent the thought process of intellect. Physical water can be solid as in ice. It can be a gas when it is agitated by heat as in steam. As liquid water has no form of itself but will assume the form of any mold into which it is poured. So it is with thoughts. They will take the form of images that are supplied by the consciousness of Man. These forms have a greater or lesser permanency depending on their relation to archetypal images, the emotional power associated with the form, the number of people imaging, and the duration of the period it is imaged.

The nature of water is further revealed by its reflectivity. When water is polluted or disturbed, the

THE HERMETIC QABALAH

reflected image is distorted. The mind when agitated, disturbed, or impure cannot reflect the inner reality. Only when the pool of consciousness is stilled and purified can the true reflection on the One Self be perceived. One of the purposes of meditation is to "still the pool."

Yesod

Yesod means Foundation. It is considered the seat of the vital soul, which humankind shares with all manifestations of life. It corresponds to the Moon, and along with Tiphareth to the Ray of Love. Macrocosmically, this Sephirah refers to the Astral Plane, that state or vibration that is contiguous to the physical plane. The Astral Plane holds the mold or matrices of the physical. Most of our imagery, fortunately, never comes to fruition in physical manifestation. For this reason, one of the titles of the physical world is Cholem Yesodoth, or Breaker of the foundations. Microcosmically, Yesod is assigned to the subconsciousness.

Malkuth

As Kether is considered to be the root of the tree, Malkuth is the fruit. Malkuth translates as Kingdom, but sometimes is referred to as "The Bride." Macrocosmically, this Sephirah is symbolic of the physical plane, the manifested universe and the Garden of Eden.

Microcosmically, it is the physical body, the Temple. Poetically it has been referred to as "The Harp of Ten Thousand Strings." The metaphors of the Kingdom

THE HERMETIC QABALAH

being restored to the true King (Tiphareth), and the bridegroom (Tiphareth) rescuing his bride, both refer to the union of the personality with the Higher Self. Until this union, Man identifies with his mortal, transitory shell. Thus, the Hebrew word for the physical body is "Guph." From it we get the term "Goofy" for one who is only a body, a dull clod.

Malkuth is normally divided into four quadrants each bearing the symbol of one of the four ancient elements.

Diagram #3   Malkuth

These elements refer to components or states of matter rather than classification of types of elements according to their atomic number.

Thus, in physical terms, Earth refers to solids, Water to liquids, Air to gasses, and Fire to radiant energy. These same qualities are seen in people who may be as stable as Earth, as flexible as Water, as active as Air, or as strong as Fire.

THE HERMETIC QABALAH

This is the merest summary of the qualities of the Ten Sephiroth. We will examine them in more detail highlighting their mystical nature later in this book.

THE HERMETIC QABALAH

Chapter 7

The Master Pattern

The spiritual aspirant must seek to comprehend the nature of the Tree of Life and its uses in the theurgical process before seeking to awaken the power symbolized by the parts represented by its individual components. By meditating on the master pattern, we find that not only does it serve as a mystical blue-print for our quest for inner knowledge, but also a powerful tool for training the consciousness in that very important relational thinking. In this way, the conscious mind becomes "in-sync" with the subconscious and a type of integration occurs.

Modern physics has proposed that the universe originated when the singularity (that point that contained everything) reached critical mass and overloaded resulting in a cosmic explosion. They term this event, "The Big Bang." All of the matter was created, according to this theory, within less than a second.

Ancient Qabalah essentially agrees with this theory (or perhaps we should say modern physics essentially

THE HERMETIC QABALAH

agrees with ancient Qabalah). It states that the energy of the ALL centered itself in what was called the Primal Point. The ancient Hermetic text, which was probably composed in Alexandria and is known as the Chaldean Oracle, says:

> ...From that paternal fountain of insupportable light it flung forth in re-echoing roar.

This is a fairly eloquent description of the "Big Bang." How the ancient Hermeticists happened on this concept is intriguing but must remain the subject for another book.

The title Primal Point is assigned to the first Sephirah of the Tree of Life, named Kether. As we pointed out earlier, Kether is the Hebrew word for Crown. And since a crown rests on (above) the head, it infers authority derived from above or before. Kether is also assigned the title of "beginning of the whirlings." Note it specifies the beginning, which is the initiation of the whirlings, not the whirlings themselves. This perfectly agrees with the supposed role of the singularity in the big bang.

The second Sephirah of the Tree is Chokmah or Wisdom. Solomon asked God for Wisdom, and God told him that he could aspire to nothing higher. Chokmah is the radiating forth of the Universal Energy. In reference to the Big Bang theory, it describes the expansion of the matter of creation, although it should be noted that this expansion does not occur in straight lines.

THE HERMETIC QABALAH

Binah, the third Sephirah of the Supernal Triad, is assigned to the feminine and magnetic force of attraction. This power of attraction of each component of the creative light, energy and matter, released by the singularity causes the circular, whirling motion observed by astrophysicists even today.

The Qabalists used the image of a lightning flash to impart the idea of the instantaneous manifestation of the attributes of the Sephiroth of the Tree of Life. According to this doctrine, Chokmah is the Divine Will that impregnates the Cosmic Womb (Binah). This gives birth to all manifestation. The first three Sephiroth, Kether, Chokmah, and Binah, serve as the first trinity and complete the Supernal Triangle of the Tree of Life:

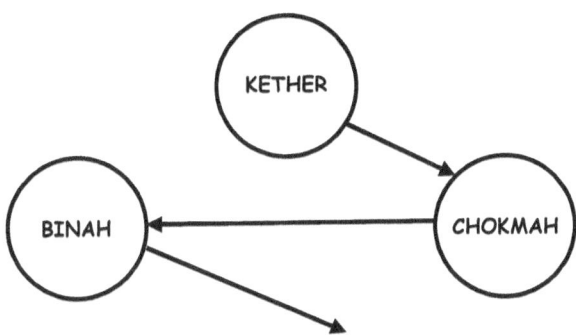

Diagram #4   The Three Supernals

The above diagram shows the Three Supernal Sephiroth and their relation to the Lightning Flash.

THE HERMETIC QABALAH

These are the roots of the Qabalistic tree which are conceived to be growing out of heaven. From these roots, the lightning flash continues, establishing the remaining seven Sephiroth.

First, are established the Egoic or Triangle of the Higher Self (diagram #4): Chesed, Geburah, and Tiphareth (Mercy, Severity, and Beauty). This triangle mirrors the Divine Triangle of the Supernals. It is centered in Tiphareth (Beauty) which symbolizes the attributes of the Sun, conceived to be a reflection of God in Kether.

Tiphareth is also referred to as the Mediating Intelligence and to the role of the Redeemer. It is linked to the archetypal "Adam." While this name is often used to refer to an individual, the Qabalists define Adam as "humanity," and therefore, it is symbolic of the Divine Light which is hidden in each one of us. It is this light, this link, which connects the human to God, the finite with the infinite.

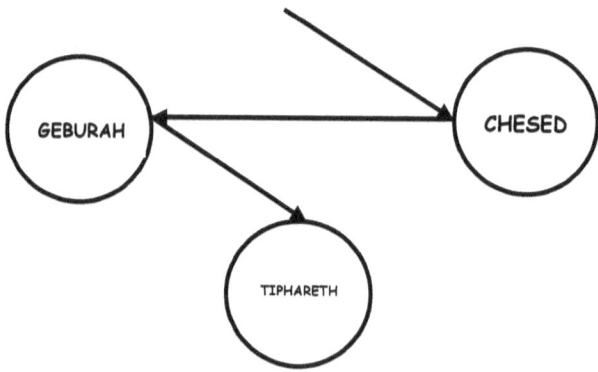

Diagram #5   Triad of the Higher Self

THE HERMETIC QABALAH

The next triad activated by the Lightning Flash is the Triangle of Personality.

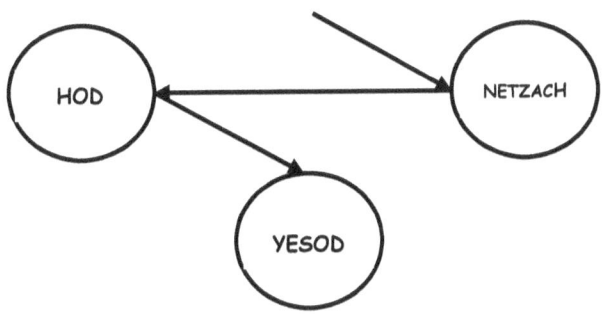

Diagram # 6   Triad of Personality

This is comprised of the seventh, eighth, and ninth Sephiroth of Netzach (Victory), Hod (Splendor) and Yesod (Foundation).

These three Sephiroth represent the macrocosmic rays of Power, Wisdom, and the Astral Plane.

Microcosmically, they correlate with the components of human personality. Netzach corresponds to the desire-nature and the emotions, Hod relates to the intellect with its image-making power, and Yesod to that vast repository of memory and fantasy known as the subconscious mind including the Collective Unconsciousness.

THE HERMETIC QABALAH

The Lightning Flash terminates in the tenth Sephirah called Malkuth the Kingdom, which represents the manifested universe.

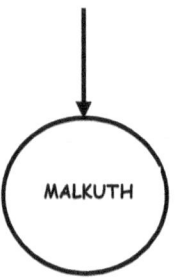

Diagram #7   Malkuth

It is important to note that no single Sephiroth is considered more holy or spiritual than any other one. They all exemplify methods by which the human consciousness may apprehend the Divine. The root of the Tree, Kether, is not closer to the Divine than is the fruit, Malkuth. In fact, as we have pointed out, this is emphasized in the classic Qabalistic text, *The Zohar*, where it says:

> ...Kether is in Malkuth and Malkuth is in Kether, but after a different manner.

The trained Qabalist strives to perfect the Kingdom, the manifested expression of time and space, by becoming a fully conscious co-creator with God. Thus he assists in bringing the primal will of Kether into Malkuth. The more completely we center our identity and consciousness at the level of our True, Higher Self in Tiphareth, the more completely we become the "Mediating Intelligence," which redeems the world. We

THE HERMETIC QABALAH

then bring the state of perfect love into our world of conditions, appearances and effects.

> ...It is to be able to love while in the midst of the turmoil of conflicts, and appearances of selfishness in incarnate existence, that constitutes true spiritual advancement."
>
> -Reverend Ann Davies

THE HERMETIC QABALAH

THE HERMETIC QABALAH

Part II

The Lesser Mysteries

The Sephiroth of the Personality

THE HERMETIC QABALAH

Chapter 8

The Kingdom

Malkuth is the Hebrew word for Kingdom. It is closely related to the words Malka (Queen) and Melekh (King). Jesus in his teachings as narrated in the Christian New Testament makes numerous references to the "Mysteries of the Kingdom." Each of these references deals directly with the subject of initiation and Apotheosis, that is, transformation into something more than Man.

Many systems of mystical teaching, especially those originating in the East, encourage the aspirant to withdraw from the world in order to pursue enlightenment in the solitude of an ashram or monastery. The Qabalah does not. One of the cardinal principles of the Western Tradition is that while you may receive mystical revelations on "the mountain top," they are not truly yours until you can prove it in the "marketplace."

Therefore, the first stage on the Path of Return, as the initiatory path is sometimes referred, is the physical

THE HERMETIC QABALAH

plane of expression. This is called Malkuth, and it is the fruit of the Tree.

In many Western initiatory systems the grade associated with Malkuth is termed Zelator. This word refers to the quality of zealous aspiration that is a prerequisite for any initiate who wishes to tread the way of mystical transformation. This zeal is much more than curiosity. It is the inwardly inspired, burning motivation to serve as a vehicle for the healing of the nations, also referred to as The Great Work. This Great Work is the spiritual regeneration of all of humanity by the perfecting of its individual members.

This zeal often results in a personal dedication to make the spiritual quest top priority. The pursuit of self-discovery becomes the purpose of daily experience. Everything we do, think, feel and experience becomes fodder for illumination.

Starting with our physical vehicle and its arena of expression, we discover the place where the work of the Qabalist is initiated. We begin with the world of time and space, but we go deeper, not content to merely accept appearances at face value. We penetrate the veil of effect to seek the cause. The zealous Qabalist begins to understand hidden laws manifesting the phenomena of our daily lives.

At this level, we begin by examining and fine tuning our sensory interpretations. Everything we know of the physical universe is transmitted to us through our senses. However, it is important to remember that it is our consciousness that interprets what we perceive. For example, we do not hear with our ears. The ears are just specialized nerve receptors for converting sound vibrations into nerve impulses. These are, in turn, transmitted to the brain which is the true hearer. This input is then interpreted by our consciousness. That being said, however, the physical senses still remain our primary interface between our environment and that consciousness. As such, it behooves the spiritual aspirant to fine tune these perceptions, which generally takes practice.

As Conan Doyle's character Sherlock Holmes demonstrates, our powers of observation can be heightened and refined far beyond that exercised by the average man or woman. By exercising this power, we can detect the interrelationships that link all aspects of life and begin to connect them together to reveal universal patterns.

We must develop "first-day awareness." This is what is hinted at by Jesus' admonition that to, "enter the Kingdom of Heaven we must become as a little child." [*Matthew* 18:3] As adults we often fall under the delusion of the familiar. We have experienced something so often that we fail to really look at (and into) it anymore. We often take our daily experiences for granted, instead being wrapped up in the banalities of conflicts and distractions. A child, however, will see the miracle of experiences because his/her vision is not yet clouded with preconceptions. All possibilities are open to the thrill of the moment. As the song writer Cat Stevens reminds us, "Morning has broken, like the first morning." [Eleanor Farjeon, "Morning has Broken"]

THE HERMETIC QABALAH

All potential is there waiting to be tapped, to experience, to transform. That which we see daily fails to hold our attention. The Qabalistic opposites, Life and Death, are appropriately associated with the power of attention. That to which we give attention, to that we are alive. With the zeal of youth, we exercise in a penetrating manner our attention and discern the inner pattern of living consciousness residing within all forms and appearances.

Malkuth is the Kingdom, but it is also related to the Bride, or Queen. The King cannot assure his future through his heir without his Queen. The King is associated with Tiphareth, the sixth Sephirah. To this Sephirah is attributed our higher and true Self. Malkuth, the material universe and our physical body becomes the area in which we express the ruler-ship of our true Self. The Queen symbolizes all powers of consciousness through which this ruler-ship expresses and takes form.

Through an enlightened manifestation of these innate powers the Qabalist brings about the new world symbolized in the Bible as the New Jerusalem, the redeemed and evolved Garden of Eden. This is also depicted as the completed Temple of Solomon.

We are privileged to live in a time when our modern scientific community is daily confirming the truths of the ageless wisdom. These "rediscoveries" when directed by enlightened men and women of integrity, will help us triumph over age-old lies and challenges of war, famine, disease and greed. On the microcosmic level, our

THE HERMETIC QABALAH

physical bodies will be modified in subtle ways until we stand forth as luminous expressions of the image of the Divine.

Each Qabalist should then familiarize herself with the latest breakthroughs of modern science. She should strive to understand the laws by which the physical world operates. Care should be taken not to neglect the ancient hermetic teachings. Each should study that amazing book *The Kybalion*, by Three Initiates. From these sources we build a foundation of knowledge with which to build our temple of illumination.

Diagram #3 on page 49 depicts the conventional symbol of Malkuth. Note that it is divided into four quadrants. Each of these parts contains one of the ancient symbols of the four elements, an elemental triangle:

$$\text{Earth} = \overline{\triangledown} \qquad \text{Air} = \overline{\triangle}$$

$$\text{Water} = \triangledown \qquad \text{Fire} = \triangle$$

Diagram # 8   The Components of Malkuth

Aristotle taught that the world was so divided. Modern Physics essentially agrees but uses different terms. They classify these expressions as Radiant Energy (Fire), Liquids (Water), Gases (Air), and Solids for the element of Earth. But, as the Hermetic Wisdom stresses, these four are really one. Every physical form

THE HERMETIC QABALAH

is actually a manifestation of innumerable points of light. This vision of radiant light comprising all things is understood by the aspirant as one of the goals of alchemy. It is what the alchemists' term, "The discovery of the First Matter." This experience is the goal of all Zelators.

Malkuth, as the fruit of the Tree, is the arena of expression for all the realizations of the other, "higher," Sephiroth.

Each of the Ten Sephiroth of the Tree of Life is traditionally associated with a Magical Image. These are Theurgical Contact Symbols that can be used to attune the consciousness to the energies of the corresponding Sephirah.

To use the diagrams, first color each one according to the instructions provided. The final product should then become the focus of a five-minute, daily meditation, to be performed at the same time each day for a period of one week. Care should be taken not to exceed the time limit, at least initially, to guard against over emphasizing the qualities of one Sephirah over another, which can produce an imbalance in the consciousness. Rather, it is advised to meditate on each image one at a time in rotation. This should produce the best effect.

Coloring Instructions

The first of these Magical Images is connected with Malkuth. The colors traditionally associated with this Sephirah are as follows: Yellow, Citrine, Olive, Russet, Black, Black flecked with Gold, and Black with Yellow

THE HERMETIC QABALAH

rays. These colors and their complements, together with flesh colors, should be used as desired by the student to color the diagram.

The "frame" should be colored as follows: Upper Quadrant, Citrine; Lower Quadrant, Black; Left Quadrant, Russet; and Right Quadrant, Olive.

In the next chapter we will discuss the ninth Sephirah, Yesod.

THE HERMETIC QABALAH

The Kingdom of Spirit is embodied in
my flesh.

Diagram #9   The Magical Image of Malkuth

THE HERMETIC QABALAH

Chapter 9

The Foundation

The ninth Sephirah, Yesod, is many times identified with the Qabalistic World of Yetzirah. It serves much the same purpose.

As the name Yesod, the Foundation, infers, this aspect of the Divine acts as the matrix on which the material universe of Malkuth is based. Microcosmically, it is both the personal and the Collective Subconsciousness.

The Collective Subconsciousness, a term derived from Carl Jung's Collective Unconsciousness, refers to that level of mind below the threshold of the conscious mind. It contains all of our memories, the workings of our autonomic nervous system, and more. At the collective level it also connects us with the memories, myths and images of all consciousness, be it human or animal, and is therefore considered the seat of the Vital Soul.

THE HERMETIC QABALAH

It is the level of the mind that mystics experience when they enter trance states and visit the "Astral Plane" or ascend the "Seven Heavens" in the Divine Chariot, etc. Great knowledge can be derived from these internal journeys. Experiences can be had that can lead to illuminating realizations. Conversely, if unbalanced and undisciplined, these activities can lead to delusionary visions and the seeker becomes lost in his personal fantasies. The Chaldean Oracles warn:

> ...Stoop not down into that darkly splendid world...for therein is established the throne of an evil and fatal force...

Yet it is this level of awareness that holds the wisdom of the ages. It has been called the Akashic Records or Library. However, as with all libraries, there are books of differing opinions and differing qualities. Some are based on truth, some on ignorance. It requires discrimination to know which is which. We should keep an open mind and root out and eliminate those based on lies.

Man shares the Vital Soul or "Nephesh" with all the kingdoms of nature, animal, vegetable, and even mineral. All of these levels have a degree of consciousness. As the Qabalistic aphorism says:

> ...Consciousness sleeps in the mineral, dreams in the vegetable, wakes in the animal and manifests in the human.

It is important to realize that all consciousness, at any level, obeys the Law of Suggestion:

THE HERMETIC QABALAH

> All levels of consciousness below the level of human subconsciousness are controllable via suggestions originating from levels above it. Human subconsciousness is perfectly amenable to suggestions originating from the level of human self-consciousness.

Yesod is the "Sphere of the activity of the Moon." Key number 2, The High Priestess, of the Major Arcana of the Tarot is attributed to this lunar quality. On the Tree of Life it is assigned to the 13th Path of Gimel, connecting the first Sephirah, Kether, to the sixth Sephirah, Tiphareth. This path bears the title: "The Path of the Uniting Intelligence." It links, once again, the ideas of Unity because unity is also, by Gematria, symbolized by the number thirteen and the Hebrew word for unity, "Achad." This is spelled A = 1 + Ch = 8 + D = 4; or 1 + 8 + 4 = 13.

This "lunar substance" forms the matrix for all things manifesting on the material plane. Remember, the Emerald Tablet tells us, "And as all things are from One, by the mediation of One, so all things have their birth from the One Thing by adaptation." This one substance is currently being studied by modern physicists. Their findings confirm the teachings of the ancient Hermetic philosophers. That is, the actual presence of energy, a single, vibrating, *conscious* energy that holds the foundational matrix of everything in the Universe. Wherever we look, every sound we hear, the objects and forces we experience on the physical plane have their origins in the world of mind, known as Yesod.

THE HERMETIC QABALAH

It is from this level that the creative consciousness of Man selects from the many images stored there, the mental constructs that become embodied in the world of form. The human spirit created in the image and likeness of the One Creative Spirit acts as a mediator or conscious transmitter through which the power of this energy manifests.

This "marriage" of energy and form that occurs at the level of Yesod is one reason that this Sephirah is assigned to the sex-organs on the Archetypal Man, known as "Adam Kadmon," in the Qabalah.

Yesod, the Hebrew name of this Sephirah, meaning the Foundation, can be pronounced slightly different to become "Yah – Sode", which means "the secret seed." This highlights the ancient mystery teaching that states that the energy that expresses in the reproductive act is also expressed through the vehicle of mental creation. Further, this same force may be adapted or modified and channeled to transform an ordinary spiritual aspirant into a fully, conscious adept.

This power is designated in the Qabalistic classic, *The 32 Paths of Wisdom*, by the name, "Sakel Tahoor" or the Pure/Clear Intelligence. This highlights the idea that this substance is ever virgin and also that the substance is perfectly responsive to the images impressed on it by the imagination. In fact, the Great Lies (or Sins) have their origin in the ignorant misapplication of human imagination over the centuries. Every interpretation fostered by ignorance and misperception have reinforced

THE HERMETIC QABALAH

these lies until they have become deeply engrained in our Collective Unconsciousness.

But, as has been observed by Paul Foster Case, this level also holds the patterns of the Wise and their accurate interpretations. Just like a vast library, we may select which authors we study. Depending on that selection, we find our responses changing and transforming our experience of reality.

This has a direct bearing on the ideas associated with what was earlier mentioned as "the secret of the seed." This is because the ideas associated with the reproductive urge are some of the most powerful that we can consider. Centuries of misuse of the consciousness and the imagination have left many deep-seated patterns of shame, guilt, and aggression. These lies critically restrict our use of this power to evolve ourselves into an illuminated expression of the Cosmos.

We can discipline our reactions to the ideas of sex and reproduction. This is not done by repressing this marvelous gift of God, but by sublimating our reactions so that they reflect a sacramental attitude. Thus, the Qabalist "lifts-up" his ideas and expressions as an offering to his Higher Self for the great work of redemption. This is Yah-sode, the secret of the seed.

This is reinforced by the Hebrew title associated with the grade of initiation attributed to this Sephirah. It is "Baal ha-Daath" or Master of Knowledge. The knowledge here referenced is not mere intellectual knowledge. Rather, it refers to the biblical meaning where knowledge is defined as, "to become one with or

THE HERMETIC QABALAH

union." This is what the Greek Hermeticists called "Gnosis."

When we start to tread the Path of Initiation and take our evolution in hand by deliberately disciplining ourselves to redirect our imagery to a more evolved, sacred attitude, we will find the great power of the Yesod level remolding our life experience into one of fulfillment.

The colors of Yesod are as follows: Indigo, Violet, Very dark Purple, and Citrine flecked with Azure. These colors with their complements and flesh colors may be used to color the Yesod diagram.

The frame should be colored from the outside frame to the inner as follows: Indigo, Violet, Very dark Purple, and Citrine flecked with Azure.

The meditational/linking practice is the same as for Malkuth, using this Yesod image as the meditational focus.

In the next chapter we will continue our study of the Tree with an examination of the Sephirah Hod.

THE HERMETIC QABALAH

In thought, and word, and deed, I rest my life,
from day to day, upon the sure
Foundation of Eternal Being.

Diagram #10 The Magical Image of Yesod

THE HERMETIC QABALAH

Chapter 10

The Divine Splendor

The eighth Sephirah is named Hod which means splendor. It is assigned to the grade of Practicus, the third grade of initiation of the Lesser Mysteries in the True and Invisible Order. The Lesser Mysteries have as their purpose the activation and balancing of the aspects of our physical/personality complex so that it may serve as a worthy instrument of our Higher Self.

The name Practicus means "one who practices." No matter how elegant a theory may be, it must be verified by practice. And mental practice or "acts of mind" must come first. Working with the energies we have contacted in the previous Sephirah Yesod, we find it absolutely necessary to purify our responses to the patterns held by the vital soul level of consciousness. This is one of the esoteric meanings behind Jesus' parable of the "Wheat and the Tares." Here he admonishes his listeners to wait until the harvest to separate the wheat (truth) from the tares (lies). He figuratively points out

THE HERMETIC QABALAH

that the place to modify these energy patterns is in the manner to which we react to their manifested forms. We must not attempt to interfere with the deep inner workings of the subconscious. This is largely ineffective at best and sometimes psychologically harmful at worst.

We must analyze the world of effects to see if we can divine in this magic mirror any symptoms of disharmony. We may safely deny that any expression of the cosmos is intrinsically evil. Appearances to the contrary are simply the temporary illusion of a work in progress. Evil is incompatible with the concept of the Unity of Life expressed in the sacred writings of all nations and epitomized in the statement in *Genesis,* "And God Saw it was good." [*Genesis* 1: 18].

Everything we experience, each trial, triumph, observation and action is a manifestation of the one creative, sustaining, transforming and redeeming consciousness. We should remember, as the Pattern on the Trestleboard states: "We are centers of expression of the Primal Will-to-Good."

The Universal Power is at our disposal because its purpose is to insure the triumph of the Great Work. Its purpose is to transform us into beings with true cosmic potential. The energy we possess is the omnipotent, omniscient, and omni-benevolent power of the creative potency of the Universe.

We must strive to embody these concepts by putting our theory into daily, hourly practice. We must follow St. Ignatius of Loyola's admonition and assume its truth by acting as if it were true. Soon, by acting it out in our

THE HERMETIC QABALAH

daily interactions, we will find this truth verified.

Remember the old Rosicrucian vow:

> ...I will look upon every circumstance in my life as a particular dealing of God with my soul.

This is the truth that will set us free.

Nothing occurs by chance. Chance is just a term for causation that is not recognized. By following the chain of causation, that is, by analyzing what cause led to our present situation and then what cause caused that, etc., we inevitably find that somewhere along the line the series was set into motion by a mental image. This is called the Law of Response.

Subconsciousness responds readily to these images applied through the right use of suggestion. It affects the mind substance, the real basis for all manifestation. This is verifiable through practice.

This is not a law that acts only sometimes or generally. It is exact and follows a definite, predictable process. Through practice we may channel the manifestation process through the activity of selecting the forms we will choose.

In fact, most of the problems we see in the world today are rooted in the indiscriminate use of the Law of Suggestion. The uncontrolled greed that results in the consuming pursuit of power and lust for money and conspicuous consumption is just one example. It is caused by the fear generated by acceptance of the Great

THE HERMETIC QABALAH

Lies of Separation, Materialism, and Mortality. These lies entered our group consciousness as a result of faulty observation, inexact analysis, and sloppy suggestions of the past.

Their solution lies in corrections made NOW. These corrections are made by conscious, persistent molding of the mental substance through correct interpretation of life experience. To gain skill in this activity requires practice. This is the practice that gives us the Latin name "Practicus" associated with this stage of the Path of Return.

The Hebrew name associated with this grade is "Baal Omen," a Master of Verity or Faithfulness. It is through regular, faithful practices that we may verify the truth of the theory postulated in the earlier grade associated with Yesod, the previous Sephirah.

Through meditation on the causal relationships of the events in our daily life we develop an increasing awareness of the essential unity and perfection of the universal order. Through one-pointed concentration on any event, we may penetrate into its essential nature and thus realize how each component fits into the universal pattern.

The ancient Hermeticists recognized what was only rediscovered in the twentieth century by our modern physicists. That is, the essential nature of all matter is light or electricity. It is this energy that expresses itself as the forms of manifestation of the Cosmic Force.

THE HERMETIC QABALAH

Further, it has been discovered, once again in accordance with ancient doctrine that this light enters into physical manifestation through geometrically identifiable patterns.

These construction forms are called "Tatwas" in the Eastern Tradition and are roughly equivalent to the "solids" of Plato.

Analysis of these forms manifested throughout nature will reveal that all of creation is based on the principles of Sacred Geometry, particularly the so-called mathematical irrationals of the ratios expressed as Pi and Phi. The latter is the basis of the famous "golden mean" and the Fibonacci Series.

Through the practice of recognizing these principles in the forms of nature, we can perceive the patterns of unity expressing throughout manifestation. This practice trains our consciousness to receive the higher principles from the sages of the Third Order.

To the Sephirah Hod is attributed all of the sciences. The essence of these subjects is reliance on the scientific method. Briefly this involves postulating a premise or a theory and making a prediction as to an outcome. The scientist then manipulates a variable and observes whether the prediction is manifested. The variable is altered and, once again, the results are observed. The experiment is repeated, attempting to replicate the results.

For example, ice is heated to 32 degrees Fahrenheit and turns to water. This is repeated under controlled

THE HERMETIC QABALAH

environmental conditions one hundred times with the same results. We can, therefore, say with reasonable certainty that the melting point of ice is 32 degrees.

Practice (testing) should always be used to confirm theory. If it doesn't confirm, scrap the theory.

Qabalistically, Hod is attributed to the planet Mercury symbolizing our intellect. Hermetically, however, especially in alchemy, Mercury is the principle associated with the higher mind and is assigned to the sixth Sephirah Tiphareth on the Tree of Life. This is a clue that the practices associated with Hod are designed to make the intellect open and responsive to the guidance of higher mentation of the true Self.

What are the practices?

First, following the advice of Saint Ignatius, we must act "as if" the level of Superconsciousness is a reality, at least to the point of keeping an open mind. Then act as if we are channels for our higher self.

Some schools advocate the setting aside or by-passing of the intellect. However, the Hermetic/Qabalistic school expresses the view that rather than eliminating the intellect, which the Life-power has spent millennia developing, we should hone it to a high degree so that it becomes a powerful instrument to achieve our goal of transformation.

However, it is in the disciplined observation of the events of daily life that the Qabalist gathers the data necessary to establish the strong intellectual foundation

THE HERMETIC QABALAH

for informed faith. This faith established on observable facts, is much stronger than the blind "belief in things not seen," that is often the stock response of the religionist.

As a product of this conscientious observation of daily phenomena, we become aware of the pattern of unity and inner causation that helps counteract the delusions rooted in past misinterpretations of sensory experience. Then the inertia of the Collective Unconsciousness, formerly an adversary, starts working for us in our search for truth.

This practice moves us away from the lie of outer causation. This lie places us in a reactive mode. Instead, the reality is that all events and circumstances are rooted in an inner mental foundation that we may proactively direct.

This transition doesn't happen all at once, but if practiced consistently and persistently our subconscious will reach a stage of crucial mass where the transformation will increase exponentially.

In addition to this practice, the Hermetic Qabalist can implement the daily discipline of active aspiration. This involves the idea that our personality is the vehicle for channeling the expression of a much higher consciousness. Today this higher level is known as the "Individuality," but has been denoted by the term "Holy Guardian Angel," in some of the older texts.

Once this concept is firmly fixed in mind, the aspirant then makes it a consistent practice, several times a day,

THE HERMETIC QABALAH

to mentally and emotionally reach up to this higher level for guidance.

This leads to what is called "Knowledge and Conversation of the Holy Guardian Angel," which today we explain as attaining to union with our essential, Higher Self and expressing that elevated realization.

Our mentally seeking guidance should be persisted in until it becomes a reflex—almost automatic. Thus we prepare the "power paths" (the patterns of consciousness) that will channel the increased energy developed in the next Sephirah Netzach. This training leads to attainment of a state of inner equilibrium that helps us maintain a firm center or anchor in the midst of the storms of daily life.

Remember Jesus' parable of the Wise and Foolish Builders? Here, we will recall that he teaches that only the Wise Builder who builds his house upon the rock will weather the storm. Thus, only the aspirant who builds his foundation with the guidance of the True Self will have the stability to withstand the channeling of potent transmutational forces. All others will be washed away.

The result for us is inner peace and serenity. During the phase of training represented by this Sephirah, we learn to mold our mental substance so that it will become the matrix of manifestation, and we can, at will, hold desired patterns in our imagination. We therefore gain skill in manifesting mental creations that later embody the fulfillment of our desires.

THE HERMETIC QABALAH

Sacred Geometry is one of the subjects studied at this stage. Through knowledge of this subject we learn about the principles of proportions and ratios on which all forms are based. No matter how complex, how complicated the outer form of any manifestation may seem, they are all based on the simplest of forms expressing these basic ratios. Most of these ratios are expressed, as we have before noted, in the values of Pi and Phi. The Qabalist should strive to see these forms that are present all around him. This process helps to develop a consciousness of the unity of all creation.

I recommend that the aspirant procure a copy of the Disney short feature, "1959 Donald Duck Donald in Mathmagic Land," (this can be seen in its entirety on YouTube). This animated short is excellent in illuminating this concept.

The colors of the frame of the image from outside to in are as follows: Violet-Purple; Orange; Russet-Red; Yellowish Black flecked with White.

Any combination of these colors or their complements with the addition of flesh-tones may be used to color the figure at the center of the picture.

THE HERMETIC QABALAH

I look forward, with confidence, to the
perfect realization of the eternal
Splendor of the Limitless Light.

Diagram #11   The Magical Image of Hod

THE HERMETIC QABALAH

Chapter 11

The Victory

The seventh Sephirah of the Tree of Life is called Netzach, "Victory." The number seven traditionally is referred to as the perfect number. Its associations in ancient and modern cultures are endless. Seven is the number to throw on the initial toss of the dice, the so-called "natural." There are seven days in the week, seven alchemical metals, seven archangels, seven chakras, and seven ancient planets. It refers to the completion of a cycle, the climax of a process. In the system of initiation represented by the Fraternity of the Hidden Light, the seventh grade of initiation is the grade of Philosophus and is associated with this Sephirah. It is the last grade of the Lesser Mysteries and represents the completion of the preparation of the personality to be a suitable instrument for the expression of the Higher Self, the Individuality.

THE HERMETIC QABALAH

Where Hod with its training of the imagination represents the foundation of the building of forms for the Hermetic Qabalist, Netzach is the basis for bringing these forms to life in both mystical aspiration and the world of manifestation.

This is because Netzach represents the desire nature. Desire is the fuel that powers the engine of aspiration. For this reason Louis Claude de Saint Martin, the 18th century "Unknown Philosopher" from whom the Society of Martinists takes its name, always referred to seekers and initiates as "men and women of desire." What he was emphasizing is the extreme importance of aspiration.

As my teacher once told me, "Desire is at the core of manifestation." Every desire will, with persistence, fuel the process of manifestation. The results will always be "victorious." No matter how it is viewed, as either beneficial or the contrary, the result will always represent a learning opportunity and progress toward enlightenment.

The aspiring Qabalist must turn away from selfish desires based on the Lie of Separation and dedicate herself to experiencing unity based on service to the highest. Jesus referred to this transformation when he admonished his disciples to store their riches in heaven, instead of where thieves could steal them and where they would rust.

This purification of the desire nature requires vigilance, the disciplined regular refusal to give expression to the patterns of selfishness, greed, and fear. When we find ourselves expressing these qualities we should analyze and internalize the situation to find the root image or emotion. We can then calmly and gently turn the imagination to visions and outcomes based on the eternal truths.

In Mabel Collins' little book, *Light on the Path*, disciples are advised to "kill out desire." Yet just a paragraph later, they are advised to desire strongly. What is the rationale behind this contradiction?

Desire may present to us many forms of expression. In itself, it is forever pure. It is an expression of the power of love. This may be difficult to accept given that the human imagination at times perverts and twists this sacred energy into forms that we find repugnant. However, at the center or core of these images created by these misbegotten children of human hatred and ignorance, lies the energy of the Divine. How could it be otherwise? There is no energy other than the One. Sometimes we must cleanse its expression from the filth of greed and selfishness, but when it is cleansed and realigned, we will find it to be a vehicle for the love of God.

This is at the root of the oft quoted fact that some of the greatest saints started out as sinners. Look at St. Francis of Assisi for example.

When we truly desire something we will at length achieve it. This requires unreserved dedication. We cannot serve two masters. We cannot fake our desire. It must be holy and sincere.

THE HERMETIC QABALAH

As the last grade of the Lesser Mysteries, it is in this grade that the final components of our personality are transmuted and prepared as a vehicle for the Higher Self or Individuality. Since desire is associated with this Sephirah we can be sure that this critical power is key to the completion of the chalice of our consciousness in the Great Work.

As it says in the *Triumphal Chariot of Antimony*:

> ...You must take the copper and wash it until it is white. [Basil Valentine]

This alludes to the purification of our desire nature. When our subconsciousness has accepted the persistent, vigilant suggestions of harmony and unity in connection to this energy, the divine victory of the illumined soul will be at hand.

This sincere pure desire will then work in conjunction with the trained imagination, mirroring true wisdom, knowledge, and practice. Intellectual discipline must balance devotional desire. The first gives direction and form of expression. The other provides the power to manifest these forms. Working together, they serve as a vehicle of expression for the One Consciousness.

The title of the grade of initiation associated with this Sephirah is that of "Philosophus." It means "one who studies philosophy." But what exactly does this mean? Philosophy comes from the Greek "phila," which means lover and "Sophia," which means wisdom. Our philosophy is the lens or paradigm though which we interpret our experiences on the one hand and the way

THE HERMETIC QABALAH

we seek answers to the riddle of Life, on the other. Why are we here? Where are we going? Who am I?

As a Philosophus, the Hermetic Qabalist seeks to find a framework that synthesizes all that his theories have revealed to him in practice.

At this Sephirah the focusing of desire into prepared channels is emphasized. The spiritual aspirant, with his increased self-knowledge, tunes his focus to a firm, theoretical and experiential knowledge of the worlds of consciousness. He uses his experience and acquired knowledge of the laws of the worlds of consciousness to build his being into a vehicle for the Cosmic Desire, the power of Love. This heightened quality, purified and focused, becomes much more powerful and effective than that of the untrained mind.

The Qabalist embraces the alchemical dictum, "Solve et Coagula," dissolve and reform. He realizes the necessity of freeing the energy from old, imperfect forms to reuse it in a higher, purer expression of the One Will. Hence, it is the alchemical element of fire that is assigned to this Sephirah. Fire is the transforming element. It is the only element that can fundamentally change the substance with which it interacts. For this reason, fire has been used throughout the ages to symbolize the passing of a sacrifice from one world to another, from the visible to the invisible, from the material to the spiritual.

The Hermetic Qabalist who has assimilated these lessons into his consciousness is ready to become one

THE HERMETIC QABALAH

with the "Mediating Intelligence" symbolized by the redeemers of all religions and philosophies.

The colors of the frame of the image from outside to in are as follows: Amber; Emerald; Bright Yellow-Green; Olive flecked with Gold. These colors may also be used in any combination to color the image.

THE HERMETIC QABALAH

Living from that Will, supported from
it's unfailing wisdom and understanding,
mine is the Victorious life.

Diagram #12   The Magical Image of Netzach

THE HERMETIC QABALAH

THE HERMETIC QABALAH

PART III

The Greater Mysteries

The Portal & the Sephiroth Of The Individuality

THE HERMETIC QABALAH

Chapter 12

The Portal & Meeting the Dweller on the Threshold

After the advancing initiate has awakened into activity the various components of personality represented by the Sephiroth of the Lesser Mysteries, he must pause and take time for Life to balance the functioning and interrelationships of these parts so that they may work together as a harmonious whole. In the system of initiation in these pages, this is designated as "The Portal." Here, a Qabalist treads the way of balanced equilibrium and temperance to pass between the tests of Materialism and Mortality, represented by the paths of Ayin and Nun on the Tree of Life.

In every one of the great mystery religions we find tests and stories designed to provide protection and guidance for the recently departed. The Egyptian Mysteries have their *Book of the Dead*, which is really titled, "The Book of the Coming Forth by Day." The Greeks had their

THE HERMETIC QABALAH

myths of heroes undergoing adventures in the Kingdom of the Dead ruled by the god Hades.

The late Dr. James Henry Breasted, of the University of Chicago, relayed to the late Dr. Manly P. Hall, that the *Book of the Dead* was actually an initiation ritual. Thus, instead of providing guidance for a recently departed through the underworld, it provided a means to successfully pass through the ceremony for rebirth into the mysteries. Dr. Breasted supported his claim by referring to staging directions he found on two different papyri copies of the *Book of the Dead*. Even though the copies differed in age by centuries, they both contained staging instructions to be followed by the priests. It is also interesting to note that there seems to be a close correlation between the reports of those who in modern times have experienced "near-death experiences" and the broad scenarios of this ancient ritual.

The Portal process brings to the initiate of the Hermetic school the experience that has been traditionally referred to as "Meeting the Dweller on the Threshold." This event, which comes to all aspirants sooner or later, was depicted in the Mysteries' stories of Greek mythology.

In these stories, the Hero would find himself paying the ferryman to transport him across the river Styx, which was the symbolic barrier between life and death. Once on the other side, he would follow a road and come to a crossroads. This place would be guarded by a fearsome creature that was, in fact the shadow soul of the Hero. If the soul could pass this guardian, this dweller, he

THE HERMETIC QABALAH

could proceed. He couldn't do it by combat or stealth. The only way he could pass by was by redeeming his shadow by the embrace of love and the kiss of peace. (Note, this is probably the origin of the fairy tales of both the Frog Prince and Beauty and the Beast.) After this kiss the shadow would transform, and become an ally. The hero could then choose one of the three paths. The left led to Tartarus, where karma could be burned (this is roughly equivalent to the Limbo of the Catholic Church.) The right led to the Elysian Fields, if the protagonist deserved the "fields of the blessed," (a place of rest until the next life). Or finally, he could take the middle way or "Royal Road" of the Initiate, which led to rebirth and service to humankind and the Mysteries.

This is the departure point of the Lesser Mysteries that leads to what is known in the Qabalah as, "Knowledge and Conversation of the Holy Guardian Angel." This archaic language should be translated as "Union with and expression of our Higher and True Self."

It is accepted that all our personalities in their natural states are imperfect. They have strengths but also weaknesses. Areas that are active and well developed are marred by others where the potential lies dormant and psychic energy is enslaved by patterns of insufficiency, insecurity, and fear.

This construction of consciousness is the vehicle for one incarnation only. While it is true that certain tendencies may be brought forward from past lives, these usually lie dormant until awakened by the forces of Karma. Thus, to a great extent, the personality is formed in

THE HERMETIC QABALAH

reaction to outside environmental factors early in life. These factors include, but are not necessarily limited to, birth experience, genetics, birth order, relations with parents and siblings, and economics.

We might say that the natural personality resembles a house constructed in a haphazard manner without forethought or plans. All of these factors produce a structure that is, in most cases, ill-suited to act as a vehicle to channel the powerful currents of the higher tension energies for the expression of the Individuality. Indeed this is one of the other meanings of Jesus' parable of "The Wise and Foolish Builder." In Hebrew the word for stone is Ehben, which is a Qabalistic symbol for union with the Higher Self. (Eb or Ab= Father and Ben=Son).

The initiatory work undertaken by the practicing Hermetic Qabalist selectively stimulates and then rebalances each component of consciousness that forms the Personality. These, of course, are symbolized by the microcosmic attributions of the 10th, 9th, 8th and 7th Sephiroth.

It is in the Portal that the interrelationships of this complex are tuned and any remaining obstructions are cleared.

Of course, being human, there always remains some vestige (albeit in a much reduced degree) of the former imbalances. These will be dealt with more intensely in the work assigned to the sixth Sephirah, Tiphareth. The grade of initiation of this Sephirah is "Adeptus Minor."

THE HERMETIC QABALAH

The following graphics depict the imbalances that may occur between the three primary "rays" or aspects of the personality.

[1] Balanced. Adept:

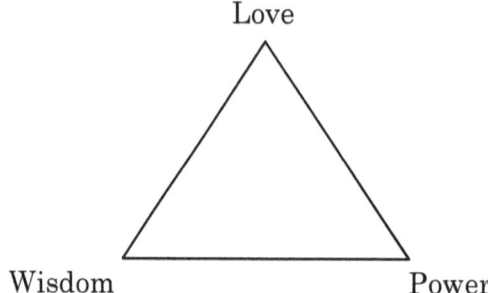

[2] Love and Power unbalanced. Undisciplined Passion:

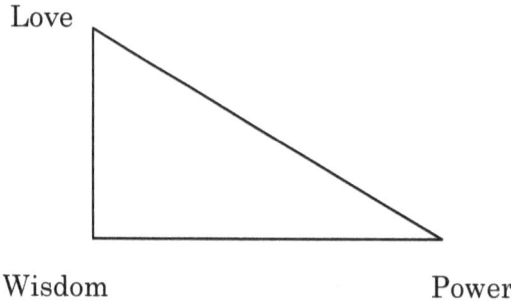

THE HERMETIC QABALAH

[3] Love and Wisdom unbalanced. Ineffective Idealism:

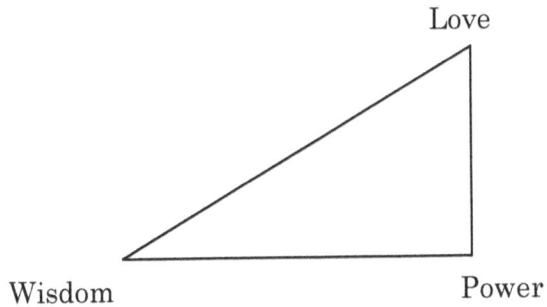

[4] Wisdom and Power unbalanced. Cold Analysis:

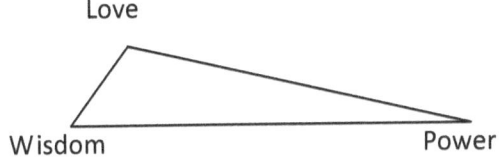

Love without Wisdom or Power = Sentimentality

Wisdom without Love or Power = Dry Intellectualism

Power without Love or Wisdom = Ruthlessness

Diagram #13   The Imbalanced Personality

THE HERMETIC QABALAH

Chapter 13

The One Ego

The sixth Sephirah Tiphareth is attributed to the Individuality and is connected with the meanings of the Higher Self. As we stated previously, the Personality is formed during an incarnation and is the vehicle of expression for that lifetime. The Individuality however is an emanation of the Solar Logos and is the vehicle of an entire evolution extending over many, many lives. The Individuality is the driver of the chariot of Personality. This process of many lives leads to a perfecting of the expression for the mediating consciousness through the gathering of skills and experiences. This mediation fulfills the phrase in the Lord's Prayer, "Thy Kingdom come, Thy will be done on Earth as it is in Heaven."

In the mystery schools of the Hermetic Qabalistic tradition there is a phrase, "Light in Extension." This refers to the fact that each Human Individuality is an emanation or "ray" of the One Light. Truly, there is

THE HERMETIC QABALAH

only one of us, expressing uniquely through each individual manifestation.

The task of the advancing initiate at this point is to strive to submit all of his personal acts, thoughts, and feelings to the guidance of his individuality. This is a practice suggested by the term, "Islam" which means "submission." This practice leads to Knowledge and Conversation of the Holy Guardian Angel, the experience of Oneness of all. It also influences the aspirant to be more compassionate, assisting, considerate, and more thoughtful in both motive and action.

To Tiphareth is assigned a three-fold Magical Image. All of the incarnations of the Holy Child are depicted here, from Krishna, Horus and Hippocrates, to Christ.

Here too, are associated the sacrificed Gods, such as Mithras, Orpheus, Osiris, and Jesus. Finally, all Messiahs or Divine Kings are attributed to this Sephirah. In all cases, at one level these are representative of the Divine Incarnation, the Hidden Light that resides in each of us.

In the Hermetic and Christian Qabalah, this is represented by the Divine name, Yeheshuah (IHShVH). This name is formed from the ineffable Tetragrammaton (IHVH). Each letter represents one of the four elements with the addition of the holy letter Shin (Sh) representing the fire of spirit. This symbolizes the fact that the presence, consciousness, love, and power of God is the essential reality of the Universe.

THE HERMETIC QABALAH

In most ritualistic presentations of the various grades of initiation associated with this Sephirah, we find the theme of death and resurrection. Each celebrates the fact of human immortality.

Even in the early church, which met in the tombs in the catacombs of Rome, this was true. It is no accident that the shape of the Christian altar was that of a sarcophagus. The priest would celebrate before an empty coffin, representing the Holy Sepulcher. The bread and wine, symbolizing the Christ was stored inside. The ceremony of the Eucharist was a ritualistic act symbolizing the resurrection of the Christ Spirit in each participant. This ceremony with its symbolic resurrection theme was an echo of the initiatory rite held in the Kings chamber of the Great Pyramid in the Old Kingdom period. The Candidate would lie down in the empty sarcophagus and the Hierophant would place him into a deep trance state. In this condition, he would be sent out onto the planes of consciousness to experience the tests and trials of the Hall of Osiris and the Judgment of Maat. Having passed successfully the "weighing of the soul" he would be awakened after three days in the tomb. Then the initiate would be "raised" by the master and travel down the ascending passage to emerge at sunrise facing the new day. Thus, he would come forth by day as one of the twice-born.

These are just a few examples of the Tiphareth formula. It can be found in Masonic, Rosicrucian, classical, as well as Thelemic systems. It is a consciousness changing, life altering event.

THE HERMETIC QABALAH

Why? Because the powerful, symbolic allegory played out to the prepared consciousness of a selected, tested, aspiring candidate causes certain key dynamics to occur.

First, the symbols penetrate deep into the receptive and fertile subconsciousness. These symbols act as if they have a life unto themselves and are as seeds, full of potential, that alter the paradigm of the aspirant's consciousness.

Secondly, they cause a shift from the materialistic doubt of a future existence, indeed a rejection of the spiritual, to an open-minded consideration of the inner world of the mind and its mysteries. This consideration of the possibility of immortality becomes a certainty when it becomes apparent that this is the only model that explains the many disparate facts that hitherto have remained, for the most part, ignored.

Thirdly, the pieces "fall together," revealing an unsuspected insight into the reality of the nature of Life. This flash of enlightenment frees a great transforming energy that literally transmutes the Qabalist into something more than he was, giving expression to the great potential that raises him above his fellows.

Fourthly, this final alchemy serves not to reinforce an elitist attitude, but rather, to convince the aspirant beyond all doubt that her destiny is the role of servant to facilitate the awakening of consciousness in all humankind.

THE HERMETIC QABALAH

With this transmutation comes the realization that, while it appears that the Personality is striving to climb the mountain of attainment, it is really the Higher Self, the Individuality that is drawing its vehicle to the summit of Illumination. He realizes that this guiding, comforting presence is always with him and is ever available to counsel and assist. Indeed, he need only turn inward and seeks its guidance.

There are others who will assist. As the inner sensorium is awakened, contact will be made with the Adepts of the Inner School or Third Order. At this level of awakening the intuition, which allows us to discriminate between the voices of illusions and the revelations of true insight, becomes more pronounced. Reception of knowledge of the inner working of the Elemental Kingdoms (those levels which comprise the consciousness behind evolution of the animal, vegetable, and mineral kingdoms) now become available. But, before the Hermetic Qabalist pursues this level of consciousness, it is vitally important that she has established a conscious link with the Individuality. Additionally, it is important to seek knowledge of these levels only through the intermediary of their superiors, the Archangels. To neglect these precautions is to risk becoming lost in the psychic delusions of the astral world. Thus, the Chaldean Oracles warn us:

> ...Stoop not down into that darkly splendid world. Stoop not down, for therein lies the throne of an evil and fatal force...

For the Hermetic Qabalist entrance into the level of Tiphareth symbolizes the attainment of the

THE HERMETIC QABALAH

consciousness of the Adept. This is union and expression of the higher consciousness. At this stage of awakening our personality and body become instruments for the Individuality. As a result of this linkage we become consciously immortal. Not belief, not intellectually convinced, although these are necessary components and prerequisites, but definite, conscious KNOWING is the hallmark of the Adept.

The attribution of the sixth Sephirah as the sphere of the activity of the Sun is apt. As the daily cycle of the sun's rising, setting, and rising again, the next day is the model for the doctrine of birth, death, and resurrection, the continuing cycle of immortality.

Yet, the experience of grief for the death of a loved one, the apparent separation, the loss, these are the emotions that encourage us to draw nearer to each other, to feel compassion for those who have similarly suffered. The adept consciously acts as a channel for the healing of these wounds and the blessing of unity and the realization of immortality.

Another attribution that is relevant is the correspondence of the metal gold to Tiphareth. Gold is called the noble metal. Symbolically this refers to the expansion of our love nature until we find the lie of separation banished from our consciousness. It requires the Qabalist to be vigilant in recognizing any tendencies toward separation and to have courage to face these patterns, root them out, and refuse to give expression to them.

THE HERMETIC QABALAH

One lie in particular is unusually seductive to the spiritual aspirant as this stage, that of spiritual hypocrisy—the dishonest tendency to express certain outward behavior as to appear spiritually evolved. This act is rooted in the personality's need to feel secure and self-important. The only solution to this situation is to humbly admit the lie, look for the root cause, and to reevaluate. This is an application of the alchemical dictum, "Solve et Coagula."

It has been expressed that in ritualistic presentations following the path of the Tree of Life that there are none above the level of Tiphareth. This is simply not true. The excuse that many of these schools use to justify this assertion is that no physical ceremony can confer the level of consciousness above the sixth Sephirah. This is absolutely true; however, the same may be said of any ceremonial degree. A ceremony merely plants the seeds. None of them bestow the change of consciousness by themselves. That is always an inner development, usually facilitated by life experiences.

Tiphareth is unique in that it has three magical images. These three tell us much, not only of this sphere of the activity of the Sun, but also about our consciousness and its changing relationship to the Self in the initiatory process.

The three images are: a child; a sacrificed god, and; a priest-king. These are connected respectively to the mythological/historical figures of Horus, (the crowned and conquering child); Jesus the Christ, as well as

THE HERMETIC QABALAH

Adonis, Mithras and Osiris; and, Solomon and the other Sun-King figures.

The Child represents the new birth of the higher consciousness in the personality. This regeneration is what is referred by Jesus in the Gospels as "You must become as a little child in order to enter the Kingdom of Heaven." *[Matthew* 18:3] It is also symbolically depicted by the children in the Tarot Major Trump, "The Sun," in many versions.

The Sacrifice God refers to the cyclic incarnations of the Individuality. This Higher Self incarnates its successions of personality vehicles into embodiment so that it may perfect itself as a conscious expression of the Divine.

The Priest-King refers to the fact that the real Self is the real ruler of our inner kingdom. This ruler is enthroned upon our heart of hearts. For the Hermetic Qabalist who is initiated into the mysteries of the inner alchemical transformative process, these three figures have obvious parallels in the confection of the Stone. Here, we may summarize it by saying three words: Bread, Blood and Fire.

The colors of the frame of the image from outside to in are as follows: Clear rose-pink; Yellow; Rich Salmon-Pink; Golden Amber. Again, these may be used in any order to color the image.

THE HERMETIC QABALAH

In all things, great and small, I see the
Beauty of the Divine expression.

Diagram #14   The Magical Image of Tiphareth

THE HERMETIC QABALAH

Chapter 14

The One Will

In the grades of initiation attributed to the Sephiroth of the Egoic Triad of Individuality the term Adept is used. In Tiphareth, Geburah, and Chesed we have the titles of Lesser Adept, Greater Adept, and Exempt Adept respectively. These grades may be represented ceremonially, but as we pointed out in the previous chapter, we should never make the mistake of assuming that experiencing the ceremony is the same as attaining the grade of awareness represented. On the contrary, a real adept will always claim to be a student.

As we pointed out in the previous chapter, the grade associated with Tiphareth is concerned with the expression and union with the Individuality, the Hidden Light within. The grade associated with Geburah has to do with identifying the personal will as an instrument for the Cosmic Will.

THE HERMETIC QABALAH

However, repeatedly in holy writings the fallacy of personal will is emphasized. Let us cite a few examples.

The word "Islam" means surrender to God and refers to surrendering to the Will of the Divine.

Aleister Crowley said, "Do as Thou wilt shall be the whole of the Law." Thou, as it is used here is a technical term in the Qabalah for the Primal or Cosmic Will.

Jesus expressed this concept with three famous quotes: "I have no will save to do the Will of the Father." "I came to do the Will of the One who sent me." "Not my will, but Thy Will be done."

This concept is also symbolized by the 12th Key of the Tarot, "The Hanged Man." In this design, the figure symbolizing the personality hangs by one foot attached to a scaffold by a white rope. This rope symbolizes the Primal Will. This card as a whole represents the disciplining of the mind. Only when we quiet the "monkey mind" of sense expressions can we "hear" the inner direction of the Divine Will.

The Primal Will is the only true will in the universe. Only when the Qabalist aligns her personality to that Will, can she truly be free. We have free choice, not free will. This is not fatalism. It is freedom.

Thus the Sephirah Geburah represents Volition to the Hermetic Qabalist. This energy is the True Will and it is cosmic in nature. It is referred to in the Qabalah as the "Radical Intelligence." Here the word "Radical" should be taken to mean as root or fundamental.

THE HERMETIC QABALAH

However, an alternate definition for radical, that of promoting change, is also relevant in regard to its connection to the sphere of the activity of Mars. This exceptionally powerful force is extremely dynamic. When channeled, it can strain the subtle vehicles of the Qabalist unless the necessary transformations of consciousness, and the alterations of the physical and subtle bodies (as discussed in connection with the transformations of Tiphareth), have been made. In fact, these transformations are absolutely necessary for the safe expression of the Mars force at this level.

Usually left-over patterns of immature responses to the Mars force create the subtle blockages that impede the flow of this powerful energy. In general these responses are connected to the Lie of Separation and its theme of selfishness. When exacerbated or left unchecked, the aspirant may even experience megalomanical tendencies. These patterns must be corrected before the Mars force can be properly channeled through the vehicle. This is accomplished by realizing that we do nothing of ourselves, but in fact it is the Father/Mother within who does all things. The small ego of the Personality must be made the instrument of the One Ego seated in the heart.

Traditionally, the Mars energy manifests through two Zodiacal signs. Scorpio, the "night-house" deals with this energy as it relates to the reproductive urge and its activities. The "day-house," symbolized by Aries, deals with the executive, transforming, and sometimes destructive functions of this same force.

THE HERMETIC QABALAH

Geburah is also known by Pachad (fear) and Din (justice). The manner in which humanity relates to this volitional energy, historically mirrors the current evolution of thought and understanding in regards to the Divine.

Primitive Man feared the dynamic Mars energy and sought to propitiate it. Later, as humankind evolved, this power was viewed as a manifestation of unyielding, mechanistic natural law or Geburian strength. Conversely, to the enlightened consciousness of the Adept, the Mars energy is realized to be a manifestation of a conscious relationship between God and Man. The term Din, or Justice, most fitly expresses this idea. The 5th statement of the Pattern on the Trestleboard clearly conveys this concept:

> I recognize the manifestation of the undeviating justice in all the circumstances of my life.

The Law of Karma is connected to the fifth Sephirah. In popular "pop" mysticism we hear the expression "bad karma." The idea is that when we experience difficulties, it is a punishment for previous transgressions. Such however is not the case. In actuality karma is a tendency toward equilibrium, harmony, and balance. The Cosmic always acts to produce a harmonious vibration—a wholeness—a unity. When our personal expression of this vibration is out of harmony we experience disease and unhappiness. The Universe then acts to bring our individualized vibration back into alignment with the whole. Karma is not punitive. It is instructive. While the experience may be painful and cause suffering, a positive conscious effort to align ourselves with the universal forces of truth facilitates the equilibrating process and lessens the negative impact.

Hence the term "adjustment" is often used in connection with Karma. It is an adjustment of disharmony and imbalance between us and macrocosmic forces. This realignment is used by our individuality to perfect its personality instrument so that we may express the Cosmic Will in ever closer perfection.

It is important to consciously participate in this process. When we do, we reinforce these patterns of harmony in the collective consciousness. This is not just an action of mind. It demands that we act with integrity, compassion, and justice in all of our interactions on the material plane.

It is for this reason that several initiation dramas (the *Egyptian Book of the Dead* being a good example), and most of the major religions feature a "Hall of Judgment." We must express Justice in our actions as well as our intentions. To stand by in the face of injustice and merely think "good thoughts" is to be the accomplice of that injustice. We must Know, Will and DARE, before we can be Silent.

Ann Davies once (to a class of students) emphasized that the alchemical (inner) transformative process alters and regenerates certain, normally dormant, organs in our physical as well as our psychic bodies. These organs, activated by the initiation process, act as mediators between the higher-levels of cosmic

THE HERMETIC QABALAH

perception and the physical level of consciousness, thereby allowing us to express much more powerful and dynamic currents of energy. Under normal circumstances, energies of this type would disintegrate the vehicles of the unprepared and uninitiated.

Reverend Davies also emphasized to her circle of students that the Mars energy is intimately linked to the reproductive energy, not only at the physical level, but on all levels and in all creatures. On the mental level this energy is expressed as an artistic impulse. It is also closely linked to the creative imagination, represented by Venus and its expression with the 14th path of the letter Daleth and The Empress in Tarot. This is one of the meanings for the mythological theme of Venus, the goddess of love being mated to Mars, the god of war. It is this mix of will and creative imagination that leads to expression of great art and also, a secret of the transformative process.

On the physical plane the Mars energy is the basis of the sexual function. However, because of centuries of expression of impure forms, this energy has been degraded into the province of pornography, "dirtiness," sin, and rape.

Rape, far from being a sexually motivated action, is a perversion of the desire for dominance and the need to compensate for feelings of weakness, guilt, and inadequacy. These immature attitudes toward what should be a sacred function must be rooted out, refused expression (mentally as well as physically) and countered by repeatedly emphasizing the holy nature of

THE HERMETIC QABALAH

the sexual function. Hierogamos or sacred sex is the attitude of every adept and should be the goal of every initiate. The true expression of this energy avoids the unbalanced extremes of both celibacy and licentiousness. Emphasis on the sacred nature of the Mars energy as an expression of the unity of all life will aid this transformation.

The Mars energy is the holy force of Awakening and is naturally related to fire as is depicted in its Tarot Key, "The Tower." Here we see the fiery power of Mars breaking down all forms based on error and false knowledge. This releases the energy trapped within these forms to perform the Great Work of Redemption.

This liberation of the trapped energy marks a very real spiritual experience usually known as "illumination." The veil of delusion is ripped away and the lie of separation is replaced by the vision of unity—if just for a moment. This vision alters the orientation of the now awakened consciousness and assures the victorious completion of the Great Work.

Many think that this awakening is the goal of spiritual practice, but they are mistaken. It is only one stage in the process of the great work of the Hermetic Qabalah. It is, however, a critical stage, for here the aspirant obtains that brief glimpse of Unity. The Qabalist becomes "a Knower of the Truth." This realization acts as a powerful seed in the unconsciousness and the inner sensorium is activated. This, in turn, leads to conscious contact with the Adepts of the Inner School also known

THE HERMETIC QABALAH

as the "Chasadim," or Masters of Compassion, the Saints or Just Men Made Perfect.

This activation is powered by the Mars energy. In the symbolism of astrology employed by the Hermetic Qabalah, it is represented, as has been mentioned by the two signs ruled by this planet, Aries and Scorpio.

In the Scorpio area, we find the reproductive organs, but there is also a connection with the Prostatic Ganglion and the inner energy center known in the East as the Savasthana Chakra. When this Chakra is awakened it causes the Divine, Holy Fire, (the nerve current known as the Kundalini), to rise up the spinal column awakening the other chakras one by one as it ascends. Finally, it enters the Aries area assigned to the forebrain and activates the higher spiritual center located there. It is variously known as the Adytum, the Throne or Zion. This is the legendary Third Eye of spiritual perception. Mars energy is connected with the beginning and the goal of the inner initiatory process.

It is the Mars force that provides the energy that fuses the serotonin in the Pineal Gland that then forms into a crystal which becomes the third eye. This physical structure interrupts and directs the higher tension astral current. This is what is known as the true Philosopher's Stone.

The Hermetic Qabalist working at this level is concerned with the concept of will and the associated concept of power. It is the proper identification and expression of the true Will that enables the practitioner to channel power effectively.

THE HERMETIC QABALAH

Many inexperienced Qabalists can unconsciously resurrect old tendencies; tendencies they thought they had long dispensed with, which then express as autocratic attitudes and inflated ego actions. The aspirant must be vigilant in recognizing and rooting out these outworn patterns. A sense of humor is essential in this battle. We must cultivate the ability to laugh at ourselves and our immature actions.

The colors used for the magical image of Geburah are: Orange; Scarlet Red; Bright Scarlet; Red, flecked with Black. Coloring instructions are the same as the previous Sephiroth.

THE HERMETIC QABALAH

I recognize the manifestation of the undeviating
Justice in all the circumstances in my life

Diagram #15   The Magical Image of Geburah

THE HERMETIC QABALAH

Chapter 15

The Master of Compassion

The third Sephirah in the triad of the Individuality is Chesed. This word means "Mercy" and, as such, it provides a balance to the severity of Geburah.

While the Hermetic Qabalist solidifies his link with his higher Self in Tiphareth, and strives to become an instrument for the Cosmic Will in Geburah, in Chesed his task is to become a channel for the unifying power of love.

The Triad of the Individuality is also referred to as the Triad of the Kings. In Tiphareth, the ruler within is seen as the mediator of cosmic forces and is symbolized as a "Priest-King." Similarly, in Geburah, it is the "Warrior-King" that is featured. Now in the Sephirah Chesed, we find the King represented as the law giver, the wise ruler, and the good shepherd. It should be noted that to be a wise ruler, a king must embody all

THE HERMETIC QABALAH

three of these aspects. He must realize the truth of all in order to express stability.

This consciousness is rooted deeply in the realization of oneness and unity, in direct contradiction to the Lie of Separation. Indeed, the title of the grade associated in the initiatory system with this Sephirah is that of "Exempt Adept." To be exempt from the last vestige of the delusion of separation is what is meant here. Jesus expressed this realization when he stated, "My Father and I are one."

Complete focusing of the entire being while still maintaining an inner balance is the hallmark of an Exempt Adept. Commitment here is key. There is no room for doubt. The Exempt Adept personifies the Unreserved Dedication. The unity of that intent is the focused work of the Primal Will of Kether.

The Hemetic Tradition links the term, "Memory" to the Sephiroth Chesed as well as the inner holy planet Jupiter. This planet is attributed to the Manipura chakra and the Solar Plexus. The arcane tradition tells us that by opening this chakra we gain access to the memory of nature, the Akashic Records. Through this recollection, the inner secrets of advanced self-evolution are obtained. Hence, the Pattern on the Trestleboard states in connection with Chesed:

> From the exhaustless riches of the Limitless Substance, I draw all things necessary, both spiritual and material.

In Chesed we find the memories of our past incarnations. The information obtained at this level

THE HERMETIC QABALAH

provides access to past skills and knowledge as well as insight into many present-day problems. By linking with these memories we are able to experience past grief, sadness, or suffering, all of which enhance our ability to empathize with others. The recollection of shared or common tests, trials, and triumphs is necessary to become a Master of Compassion.

With this common experience we are filled with the desire to alleviate the suffering of our fellow humans. And with the knowledge gained in our journey up the Tree, we can actually develop the ability to do so.

The Divine name associated with the Sephirah is, "El" or, "of God." Most of the archangelic names in fact use this suffix. For example, Raphael is translated as "Healing of God." Haniel is "Grace of God," and Auriel is "Light of God." These names suggest the root power that unites all of these aspects is the divine power of God.

When the Exempt Adept's consciousness becomes more responsive to the guidance of Chesed, a link is formed with the initiates of the Supreme Mysteries, those known as the Third Order in the Western Tradition. As a result, an initiate of this grade is said to "stride across the Abyss." Although there are many paths leading from the triangle of the Individuality, there is but one that the advancing initiate may travel to reach the higher consciousness represented by the Sephiroth of Binah, Chokmah, and Kether. This path is the Path of the Uniting Intelligence and it passes through the initiatory experience known as Da'ath.

THE HERMETIC QABALAH

The name of the Intelligence (from the Qabalistic treatise *The 32 Paths of Wisdom*) assigned to Chesed is "Saykel Oboah," which means the Recepticular Intelligence. It is based on the same verb root as Qabalah, "Qebel," which means "to receive." Oboah implies a certain sustaining power, a consistency. Chesed becomes a container of the form-producing power originating in Binah. This manifestation of receptivity is the result of the intense desire to "know" that is an aspect of the uniting power of Cosmic Love.

In Tiphareth, we become consciously immortal, identified with our eternal spirit. In Geburah, this spirit is realized to be a vehicle of the Cosmic Will. Finally, in Chesed this Will is identified as Divine Love. The statement "God is Love," becomes a verified experience.

Using the memory aspect of Chesed, in conjunction with our Solar Plexus Chakra, we may also access knowledge developed in ancient epochs of history. This is made possible via the 16th Path of the letter Vav which links this Sephiroth to that of Chokmah or "Wisdom." The Hermetic Qabalist will remember that the letter Vav is closely related to the idea of receptivity to the inner teaching. The Exempt Adept links with the knowledge and wisdom of Chokmah by focusing the desire force of Netzach.

The fifth Arcana of the Greater Trumps of the Tarot exemplifies these meanings. This figure depicts the Hierophant or inner teacher instructing two acolytes who represent the intellect and the emotions. The

THE HERMETIC QABALAH

Qabalist operating at this level fulfills Jesus' statement, "I judge as I hear..." [*John* 5:30]

The Exempt Adept is known as a Chasadim or Master of Compassion. As such, she is a channel of the infinite compassion of the three-fold Godhead, represented by the Supernal Sephiroth, Kether, Chokmah, and Binah. They represent a higher level of authority than a Qabalist working at the level of Geburah, only. A Judge (representative of the Greater Adept) may pass judgment, but he does not have the power to pardon. That privilege is reserved for the ruler acting at the level of Chesed.

The Exempt Adept is like the Bodhisattvas of the Buddhist tradition. She is exempt from the necessity to incarnate. Yet, she still chooses to do so out of compassion for the human race. She descends into embodiment that she may lighten the suffering of those still bound to the wheel life and death. Through the Exempt Adept the power of love and compassion flows from the Great Ones of the Third Order to all in need and who are receptive. Their very presence heals on all levels. Yet an initiate of Chesed will do this only when asked. For one of the requirements to receive healing is receptivity. The true Brethren of the Rosy Cross are at this level and who, it will be remembered, professed nothing save to heal and that gratis. This is also the true meaning of the Rose Cross symbol, the Rose of Love redeeming the Cross of the Sacrifice.

The colors for Chesed are: Deep Violet; Blue; Deep Purple; Deep Azure, flecked with Yellow.

THE HERMETIC QABALAH

From the Exhaustless riches of it's Limitless
Substance. I draw all things needful,
both spiritual and material

Diagram #16   The Magical Image of Chesed

THE HERMETIC QABALAH

PART IV

The Sephiroth of the Supreme Mysteries

THE HERMETIC QABALAH

Chapter 16

Across the Abyss

Between the Supernal Sephiroth of Kether, Chokmah, Binah and all of the Sephiroth, is the great symbolical Abyss. The Abyss represents the demarcation between the finite and the infinite nature of consciousness. While Man is said, in scripture, to be created in the image and likeness of God, God is not identified as Man or vice versa. In Qabalah Man's consciousness with the Divine is called "cleaving" inferring that human consciousness while perhaps essentially one of a kind, is vastly different in degree than his creator.

"Gnosis," is a type of knowing that is used to describe an immediate enlightenment that by-passes the intellect and directly illuminates the human consciousness. The authors of the *Kybalion* explain this gnosis by describing God as the ALL. It would be illogical, they explain, to say the consciousness of a human could comprehend the nature of the ALL. Comprehension means "to grasp" or "to grasp or surround a subject." The human consciousness would have to be, by

THE HERMETIC QABALAH

extension, greater than the subject grasped. In the case of the ALL, this would indicate that human consciousness is greater than or existing independent from the ALL. If this was true then the ALL wouldn't be the ALL, but merely a part. Comprehension of the Infinite is a logical impossibility.

Fortunately, there is a mode of knowing that is above the intellect and which does not depend on logic. This is Gnosis. This direct knowing has been experienced historically by many who testify in evidence to its reality. Here the consciousness does not try to grasp the ALL by comprehension, but instead seeks to apprehend or touch the essence of the infinite. This mystical touch transforms the consciousness of the aspirant by its resonant vibration (causing it to vibrate in harmony), and the consciousness perceives the cosmic inner nature.

With this experience the Hermetic Qabalist becomes the receptive vessel of the three-fold nature of the Divine. This has been described as the Creative, Preserving, and Transforming nature of God in many Eastern religions.

In the Qabalah, this is further denominated as the Creator of Being, the Creator of Force and the Creator of Form. We will discuss this in more detail in the chapters on Kether, Chokmah, and Binah. Let it be emphasized here that we are not referring to three separate deities but three different aspects of the One, the ALL.

THE HERMETIC QABALAH

Although five visible paths represented on the Tree of Life span the Abyss, it is generally taught that only one of these may be used by human consciousness to cross it, the others being reserved by different, non-human manifestations or, perhaps alternatively, used for the functioning of forces descending from the Supernals into human consciousness. For more on this the reader is directed to W.G. Gray's book, *The Ladder of Lights*, listed in the bibliography.

The path that the mystic may use to cross the Abyss is that of the 13th, known as the "Path of the Uniting Intelligence." If we explore the Qabalistic number system known as Gematria the title of this path is appropriate for many reasons (for readers not familiar with this system, you are referred to Wade Coleman's excellent work, *Sepher Sapphires*, in two volumes listed in the bibliography).

Using Gematria, every Hebrew letter serves as a number, a practice that was superseded when the now familiar Arabic numbers became the predominant system. Thus, in the early Qabalistic texts each word could be assigned to a number simply by adding the sum of its individual component letters. (See Diagram #1 page 26)

The number 13, assigned to this path has many illuminating correspondences. We will mention just three in connection with this discussion.

    (1) BHU – Bohu – a void or an abyss.

    (2) AChD – Echud – Unity (Union).

THE HERMETIC QABALAH

(3) ABVH – Ahevah – Love.

These references to the Path of the Uniting Intelligence are indeed appropriate and obvious. The Abyss or void is a place of all possibilities where ideas proceed from the One Source to manifestation. It is the path of union with the Divine. This path or discipline is referred to in the East as Yoga. God, the Source is love in His/Her innermost essence, the force which unites.

It is on this path that the Aspirant encounters the mystical, quasi-Sephirah known as Da'ath.

Many authors (W.G. Gray, for example) question whether or not Da'ath should be considered a Sephirah at all. Others of the school of Chabad (a Jewish Qabalistic school) advocate its inclusion.

The whole controversy revolves around a statement found in the Qabalistic classic, *The Sepher Yetzirah*. This book is one of the earliest works on the Tree of Life. Here we find the assertion, "There are ten Sephiroth, ten and not nine, ten and not eleven." Seems unequivocal, doesn't it? Yet, on the mystical way of return Da'ath seems to be a reality and a reality to be reckoned with. What is the solution to this apparent contradiction?

This answer is right in front of us. As its name suggests, the *Sephirah Yetzirah* or *The Book of Creation* or *Formation* is a book of cosmology and the involutionary path of creation. It doesn't deal with the mystical return of consciousness at all.

THE HERMETIC QABALAH

When the aspirant starts on the path of return, that is The Path of Initiation, is it possible that conditions change, that another aspect of consciousness, another realization or experience occurs that the Qabalist refers to as Da'ath?

Da'ath translates as knowledge. But, we disagree with W.G. Gray that this refers to intellectual knowledge or comprehension. As we pointed out in our discussion of Tiphareth and the Knowledge and Conversation of the Holy Guardian Angel, we believe that knowledge here refers to "Union" and the experience of Gnosis or direct knowing by touching the essence.

There is no "magical image" assigned to Da'ath. However a meditational image of the "Empty Room," traditionally connected with it does make sense as it implies a direct encounter with the ultimate representation of Deity since it is the No-Thing that which has no form and therefore, no form can define or represent It. To understand this all-potential, we must realize our Oneness with it. No intermediaries, no veils can obstruct this experience of Union.

The archangel of the element of Earth, Auriel is sometimes assigned to Da'ath. But also, and perhaps more importantly, the name (or rather title) Auriel is Hebrew for "Light of God." This is, in fact, the essence of the material manifestation of Earth. As our physicists will tell us, all matter is a manifestation of an energy that can be defined as electro-magnetic radiation or Light.

THE HERMETIC QABALAH

In the next chapter we will consider the root of form, Binah and how the Tree of Life illustrates the "Big Bang" theory.

THE HERMETIC QABALAH

Chapter 17

The Qabalah & The Big Bang

The predominant (but by no means unanimous) version of creation espoused by modern-day physicists is a theory called the Big Bang.

In the beginning, all energy and matter was concentrated in an ever-contracting singularity. In Qabalah this beginning corresponds to Kether which is referred to as the "Primal Point."

The singularity reached critical mass and exploded, creating all matter in less than a second. Qabalists use the symbol of the "Lightning Flash" to represent this phenomenon. The second Sephirah, Chokmah, said to be the root of fire, radiated outwardly from a point (i.e. Kether).

THE HERMETIC QABALAH

The magnetic power of gravity acted on this primal matter, causing the substance to whirl and expand. In Qabalah, this action is referred to as Binah, the beginning of limitation. Kether, also known as the "beginning of the whirlings," finally manifests as form through Binah.

Accordingly, the ancient Qabalah and modern physics substantially agree!

THE HERMETIC QABALAH

Chapter 18

The Womb of Creation

Binah is considered the "Root of the Power of Water."

Each of the Supernals is considered a root on the Tree of Life. Kether is the "root of air," Chokmah the "root of fire," with Binah, as we have mentioned, "the root of water." Water, of course, does not refer to material water but something which has water-like characteristics. Something that flows, has currents, dissolves, and cleanses while also having qualities that resemble ice and steam.

Water has always been a symbol for the mind and consciousness. It is the plastic medium that provides the matrix for manifestation. Hence Binah appropriately heads the Pillar of form.

Binah is also associated with the "Holy Spirit" through its correspondence to the Neshamah, the intuitive higher consciousness.

THE HERMETIC QABALAH

The grade of initiation assigned to this Sephirah is "Magister Templi" or Master of the Temple.

The Knights Templar used this title to designate the head of one of their Preceptories. This is, incidentally, very strong circumstantial evidence linking the Poor Knights of Solomon and the Temple (the Knights Templar) to the Rosicrucians and the Freemasons.

Esoterically, the Temple is the Personality and its physical vehicle. It is the Unfinished Temple. We complete this Temple by climbing the Tree. This process is known as "initiation" in the Western Mystery Tradition.

The Master of the Temple is the first grade of the Third Order, or the Supreme Mysteries. This grade can only be attained when the three grades of the Second Order, those of Adeptship, are awakened and equilibrated. Thus the tasks of the grade of Tiphareth, identification with the Higher Self; Geburah, identification with the Higher Will; and Chesed, identification with the Higher Love are completed and interacting harmoniously.

Attaining to the level of the Supreme Mysteries does not eliminate the illusion of personality limitations. This is innate when functioning in incarnation. This is still true for the Masters of the Third Order. While functioning in time and space, this is a necessary illusion. What has been overcome is the delusion of this lie.

Binah deals with the power of limitation and restriction. In the Hermetic Qabalah, this power is associated with

THE HERMETIC QABALAH

the characteristics of the planet Saturn, as depicted in astrology.

A traditional catechism is connected with entry into the Sephiroth of each of the three orders (or Mysteries) and refers to the oath or obligation taken there:

First Order:
Q: "What makes you an Initiate?"

A: "My Obligation."

Second Order:
Q: "Who is an Adept?"

A: "One who is bound by his obligation."

Third Order:
Q: "Who is a Master?"

A: "He who embodies his obligation."

Each of these stages involves a free choice to abide, bind, and embody by an agreement, a contract, an oath. It is voluntary restriction to live life in accordance with a code of behavior and principles. This restriction or limitation, taken of the initiate's "own free will and accord," enables her to focus all her energy on the transformation from natural woman to illuminated woman. An ever growing desire to be of service to humanity, the higher Self, and Truth fuels this transformation. As Dion Fortune emphasized, "I desire to know in order to serve," are the key words that open the gate of the Temple.

THE HERMETIC QABALAH

This obligation taken in the "Empty Room" of Da'ath, admits the aspiring Hermetic Qabalist into the Supreme Mysteries. This "Empty room" represents the Secret Place of the Most High. In the Bible, we see this described as the Sanctum Sanctorum or Holy of Holies of King Solomon's Temple. It was here that the high Priest bows before the Divine Presence (the Shekinah), seated on the Mercy Seat above the Ark of the Covenant, once every year to ask for forgiveness for the past year's sins of the nation. Here he also pledges his obligation to the people again for the coming year.

In the Mysteries of the Hermetic Qabalah, there is an act known as taking the Unreserved Dedication. This oath, made to your Higher Self, involves a complete dedication of every word, deed, action, and thought to the service of the highest and truest. It is an entering into a solemn contract made between the Masters and the aspirant. The Initiate offers herself totally and the Masters pledge to provide the support necessary to fulfill that obligation.

This restriction and limitation focuses on the sacred goal of universal redemption, placing service as the highest priority in life.

The name of the third Sephirah, Binah is usually translated as "Understanding." However, Ann Davies translated this word as "the power of separation." Binah is the all potential force transmitted from Chokmah, divided into the many forms of expression. As computer programmers will tell you, at each decision gate on a programming flow chart, once a choice is made

THE HERMETIC QABALAH

(yes or no), exclusion is made. There becomes a path not traveled. This is manifested in each of us as the power of free choice.

As the root of the power of water, Binah represents the Divine Mind, the Neshamah. She is sometimes spoken of as the Great Sea, "Mara," from which we get the name Mary. Mary is the mother of God in the Catholic denomination of Christianity. Appropriately, Binah is referred to as the Great Mother in Qabalah. In this connection she is also called, "The Dark Sterile Mother" (Ahmah), the Superior Mother, and the Terrifying Mother. These appellations refer, once again, to the restricting and limiting characteristic of the "form" aspect of the Divine Mind. Yet, without this limiting no creation is possible. This limitation to a field of expression relates directly to the path of the Hebrew letter Cheth, proceeding from Binah. This letter means "fence," and it is the "fence" of personality that allows the expression of any form to take place.

The Divine name "Elohim" is assigned to this Sephirah. Elohim is the name used in the first chapter of Genesis to designate the creative power. The name is made up of a singular feminine root combined with a plural masculine suffix. It therefore symbolically designates the creative power to be both the one and the many, male and female. Through Gematria we find that Elohim is related to Eheyeh-Adonai—the Divine names related to Kether and Malkuth, combined—to the whole Tree of Life. This emphasizes the fact that the creative power which creates the universe is one. This power

THE HERMETIC QABALAH

expresses from the Primal Will to the Garden of Manifestation.

Binah is located at the head of the Pillar of the Future and of Form. It is often called the Womb of Creation. This pillar is also referred to as Boaz (after the left hand pillar of King Solomon's Temple) and the pillar of strength and severity. One of its relatively unknown designations is the Pillar of the Elohim. Note the God Name of all three Sephiroth on this pillar.

    Binah = Elohim

    Geburah = Elohim Gebur

    Hod = Elohim Tzabaoth.

Elohim Gebur translates as "Lord of Strength," sometimes translated as "Lord of Armies" and Elohim Tzabaoth as "Lord of Hosts."

Often Binah is called AMH, amah, "the Dark, Sterile Mother." However, when activated by the masculine power of Chokmah (symbolized by the Hebrew letter Yod) along the 14th Path of the letter Daleth, she becomes the "Bright Fertile Mother." Symbolically this is illustrated by the addition of the Yod to Amah (AMH) transforming her into Aimah (AIMH). It is interesting to note that in the Tarot this path is represented by The Empress, which depicts a pregnant queen, who is blond (bright) and is replete with the emblems of fertility.

In connection with this "seed" illustration, there is a Qabalistic maxim, "Attention gives life!" Simply explained, it means that we reinforce and give strength

THE HERMETIC QABALAH

to whatever we allow our consciousness to give expression. The Great Lies become entrenched in our collective consciousness by countless generations of humanity misinterpreting sensory phenomena and then giving strength to that distorted view by placing our attention on these inaccurate interpretations. As spiritual aspirants, we can dissolve the power of these lies by refusing to give expression to them and by consistently placing our attention on the truth of Unity, Spirituality, and Immortality.

This does not mean we ignore the challenges placed before us and others, the ones evoked by the lies at this present stage of collective awakening. But it does mean that we refuse to give expression to the falsehoods they represent.

The Qabalist thus becomes a redeemer for all who dwell in the garden. This is what Jesus meant when he declared, "If I be lifted up, I will lift all others unto myself." [*John* 12:32]

The power of limitation represented by Binah enables the aspirant to focus her attention in a way that eliminates the unconscious expression of falsehood. Through this limitation she emerges into the expansion of liberation. She becomes a channel for the consciousness of the Cosmic.

Binah is attributed to the planet Saturn. In the Hebrew alphabet, this quality is assigned to the letter Tav (Th).

THE HERMETIC QABALAH

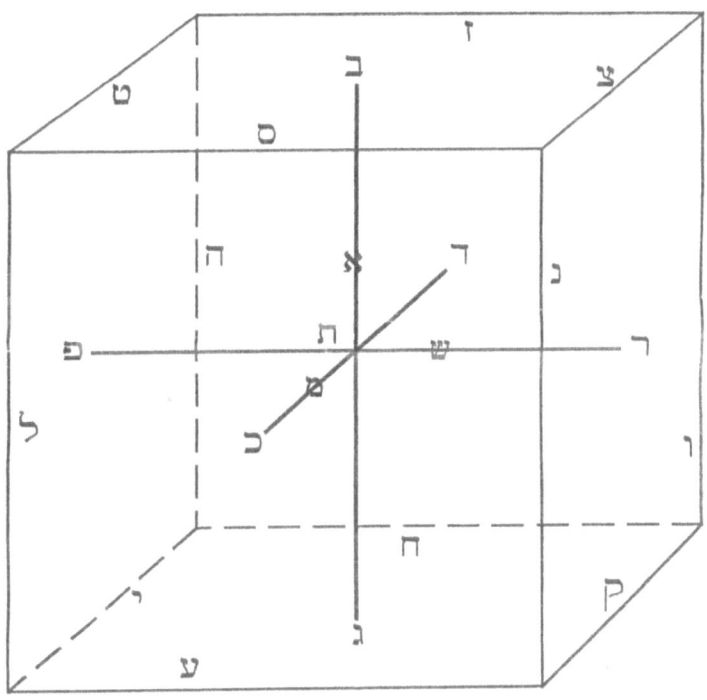

Diagram # 17   The Cube of Space

THE HERMETIC QABALAH

On the diagram of the Qabalistic Cube of Space, described in the *Sepher Yetzirah*, this letter is placed at the center of the cube. This location is referred to as "The Palace of Holiness in the Midst." Symbolically, this is emblematic of the truth that for every form, the indwelling essence is the Divine. Truly, we are all centers of expression for the consciousness of the Cosmic.

The colors for the following diagram are: Crimson; Black; Dark Brown; Grey flecked with Pink.

THE HERMETIC QABALAH

Filled with Understanding of it's perfect law
I am guided, moment by moment along the
path of liberation

Diagram #18   The Magical Image of Binah

THE HERMETIC QABALAH

Chapter 19

The Fountain of Light

In the Chaldean Oracles we read, "From that fountain of insupportable light, which none may name or define, it hurled forth in re-echoing roar."

As we pointed out in the previous chapter on "Qabalah and the Big Bang," this passage summarizes nicely the explosion that created the Universe. It also applies perfectly to the Sephirah Chokmah. Chokmah is the head of the Masculine Pillar of Force and bears the title of the "root of the Fire."

The masculine force in Qabalah is the initiatory, projective power that sets all things in motion. It is the impetus behind all activity. By it, the forms produced in Binah are stirred into activity.

While Binah produces form through the power of restriction and limitation, Chokmah is without limits. It is the expansive force containing all possibilities.

THE HERMETIC QABALAH

Qabalists refer to this energy as "Chaiah" which roughly translates "the Divine energy of the Life Power." This is reflected in one of the Divine Names attributed to this Sephirah, Yah, (IH). It is the first half of the Tetragrammaton or ineffable name of four letters IHVH, which is said to contain the entire process of creation. Yah therefore is the first half or root of creation comprising the fiery motivating seed of energy (Yod) and the form matrix or holy womb which the masculine energy of Chokmah impregnates. It is this force that transforms the sterile, dark mother, Amah, into the bright fertile mother, Aimah.

In the Eucharistic ceremonies of the Christian Church, this mating is symbolized by the wine or "blood."

Further, while Yod is definitely a masculine letter, assigned to fire, the Heh is a feminine letter attributed to the element of water. It is this quality of equilibration that enables the Qabalist to ascend and achieve the blissful experience of union with the Father. Jesus said, "My Father and I are one." In this way, Yah may be said to symbolize the ability to be receptive to the Divine Wisdom from above. However, this reception of power from the Cosmic Source is not useful unless matched with the ability to channel and embody this energy and guidance.

Tarot Key #12, The Hanged Man, symbolizes this quality. Here is depicted the suspended mind. To receive the cosmic wisdom of Chokmah, the Qabalist must have quieted the Personality into a silent, still and suspended state. The title of the grade of initiation

THE HERMETIC QABALAH

assigned here is Magus or Master. She who embodies this elevated state of consciousness has trained the personality to become a silent witness to the work of L.V.X. (light). This awareness is projected to all those who are receptive. Since these thoughts and images are the embodiment of the Life Power's energy, they are immensely more powerful than the undisciplined, unfocussed thoughts of delusion which are the domain of the Shadow. They are based on Truth and shine like a beacon in the dark night.

This beacon of light held aloft by the illumined consciousness of a Magus is more than just a marker in the darkness. Because of the qualities developed in the preceding degree of Master of the Temple the discipline of focus is now part of its expression. The diffused floodlight of benevolence has been concentrated into the laser-like beam of an active and potent tool for good. Not only can such a one feel compassion for all those who suffer, but now he or she may become an active agent to alleviate the cause of that suffering. The Qabalist who has attained the grade of Magus becomes an active, conscious instrument in redeeming a world in great need. This becomes the first priority in the life of the advancing Hermetic Qabalist. She becomes the third letter of the Tetragrammaton, the Vav.

The word Vav means nail and it serves as the conjunction "and" in the Hebrew language. The Magus serves as a link, a connection, a nail between the Cosmic (symbolized by Yah) and the rest of the manifest creation (symbolized by the final Heh of The Name).

THE HERMETIC QABALAH

The work of the Magus **is** humanity. She, with the whole of her being, directs the harmony of the Primal Will. This "harmony of the Primal Will" acts as both a catalyst, and an agent of balance, to redress misalignments in the soul of humanity and all creation. All of the faculties, skills, and talents of the higher Self become jewels in the crown of the One Life.

The Qabalist receives the Cosmic Wisdom as abstract mathematical principles. He then embroiders them through the creative imagination until they become comprehensible to the receptive consciousness of humanity.

The Divine Wisdom instructs us using the uniting aspect of nature. As my teacher once pointed out, all learning and experience leads us toward unity. Even slavery to the Great Lies teaches us lessons that when absorbed will liberate us. Pain is a potent teacher. But, for the aspiring soul treading the path of return using the path of the Hermetic Qabalist, the Way of Truth is more efficient—and more rapid. This is the path of service to the highest.

Following the inner promptings of the One Will, we experience union with that Cosmic Awareness and confirm the ancient Hermetic doctrine of, "All things are from the One." This is confirmed by modern scientific teaching such as that of "Super String or M-Theory." In this theory, all things are seen as the same in essence, manifesting differently according to different rates of vibration.

THE HERMETIC QABALAH

Those familiar with doctrines issuing from schools such as Thelema will be familiar with the doctrine of the Word. According to this teaching, every Magus expresses his inner revelation in a formula summarized and expressed as "the Word of the Aeon." Aleister Crowley, for example, declared his word to be "Thelema" or Will. Whether we agree with this particular doctrine or not, the doctrine of sound vibration has many precedents. For example, the yogi Patanjali declared that, "Through sound the world stands," [*Raja Yoga*] and stated that sound to be the essential nature of the Tatwa Akasha.

While we tend to think of sound as that narrow range of vibration we can sense with the ears, it is much more extensive. Certain of those vibrations can be received by the hearing centers in the brain of a properly trained adept and these become vehicles for the transmission of Cosmic Wisdom.

When these inner oratory centers are completed, reception of this wisdom, taken in combination with the understanding of the foundations of form learned in Binah, unite into a powerful combination. One who has made this connection is able to perform "works of power" traditionally associated with the term Magus.

The letter Yod has an interesting symbolical relationship with Chokmah. First, Yod is considered the basis or foundation of the Hebrew alphabet, also known as the Chaldean Flame alphabet. It even looks like a tongue of fire. Chokmah, as we have pointed out, is the root of the power of fire. Additionally, Yod is attributed

THE HERMETIC QABALAH

to the Qabalistic World of Atziluth, also connected with fire. There is a teaching that the upper point of the Yod is Kether (the first Sephirah), and the body of the letter is assigned to Chokmah.

Diagram # 19   The Hebrew Letter Yod

The 11th Path of wisdom connecting Kether to Chokmah is referred to as "the Path of the Fiery Intelligence." This attribution points out that the cosmic Fire of Chokmah is rooted in the hidden recesses of the Primal Will of the first Sephirah. This is further hinted at by the numerical correspondence of "Jah" to the Hebrew word "sub" which means "to flow." This relates to the "Mezla" or Divine Influence that flows like lightning from Kether to Chokmah and thence to the rest of the Tree.

In the initiatory work of the Hermetic Qabalistic tradition the thought processes stimulated by the control of the Mezla gradually builds modifications in the mental body that help in the transmittal of these

THE HERMETIC QABALAH

concepts of mathematical proportions. It is upon these concepts that the universe is based.

This is explained in statement #2 of the *Pattern on the Trestleboard*, where it states: "Through me Its unfailing Wisdom takes form in thought and word."

Human consciousness and similar manifestation elsewhere in the universe, serve as a vital vehicle for the continuing unfoldment of the cosmic plan. The consciousness of the Magus receives the divine plan from above and steps it down in vibration to be embodied in the work of manifestation. This requires persistence, deep devotion, and clear imaging. Fuzzy, sentimental and inexact thinking must be avoided. Clear, concise, defined comprehension is the goal towards which to strive. The model of Truth must be central to this work. In this way, the concept of unity is reproduced in human consciousness and the expanse of nature.

To provide a vehicle for this level of consciousness the Qabalist must not only be devoted but also be intelligent. Intellectual and emotional development is an absolute prerequisite for the work. We cannot afford to be either emotionally stunted or intellectually lazy if we wish to be channels for the Divine Wisdom. Both must be expressed in a balanced, dynamic equilibrium. Thus, and only thus, may we make of ourselves an effective channel for the flow of the evolutionary energy. Remember, at this level of consciousness, this energy manifests not as mere belief, but as direct Knowing, Sophia—Divine Wisdom.

THE HERMETIC QABALAH

This direct knowing of wisdom acts as a vehicle of transmission between the Divine and the Imagination function of the Individuality represented by Tiphareth. Through it the pattern of the Primal Will is transmitted to the consciousness of humanity.

To be effective at this level all selfish, self-aggrandizing, ego-drives must have been sacrificed or cleared from the consciousness. Only then may the Qabalist be truly a Master and a link for the Cosmic Wisdom. Such a person experiences the concepts of universal truth, not for himself only, but for all of humanity. In this way, he becomes an Avatar or incarnation of some aspect of the Supernal Wisdom.

Chokmah is assigned to the "Shamayim" or heavens, usually interpreted as the Zodiac. However it may be also related to the untrammeled, stellar imagery of space before limitation or definition contracts it into stars. The latter is represented by Binah, as the first Sephirah to be attributed to a planet. In ancient writings planets were referred to as "stars." Once again the idea of "channeling" is emphasized. The source of creative energy does not originate in Chokmah but expresses through it. Chokmah as the Cosmic Father can only be defined in relationship to Binah, the Divine Mother. Until impregnation of the womb has occurred, there is no Father. It is a role defined not by quality, but by function. The same is true for Binah. Herein is the mystery of the sacred trinity. Each part manifests separately but is, in fact, one unity. There is one!

THE HERMETIC QABALAH

Chokmah is designated in the *Thirty Two Paths of Wisdom* as the "Illuminating Intelligence." Initiates of this level transmit the gnosis of Cosmic Wisdom and illuminate the minds of all aspirants receptive thereto.

"Illuminating" in Hebrew is spelled MZHIR, mazahir, which has a gematria value of 262. This is also the value of "chadarim," (ChDRIM), which means Chambers or secret places and brings to mind the phrase "secret places of the Most High." These chambers are the inner holy planets or Chakras that figure prominently in the alchemical work of inner transformation. Particularly "the secret place of the Most High" is a reference to the Adytum, the third eye, where the Philosopher's Stone is formed. Here is awakened the inner eye of spiritual vision—the eye which perceives the oneness of all. It is the experience that the Hermetic Initiates refer to as "the discovery of the first Matter."

The task of the Qabalist in Chokmah is to identify with the Life force, Chaiah. Becoming one with the one causative power assures success in all endeavors, "If God is for us, who then can be against us?" [*Romans* 8:31] However, we should remember that one of the initiates of this level has already realized identification with the One Will. "He has no will, save to do the Will of the Father."

The colors of Chokmah used in the coloring of the Magical Image are: Pale soft Blue; Grey; Pearl Grey, Iridescent; White flecked with Red, Blue, and Yellow.

THE HERMETIC QABALAH

Through me. Its unfailing Wisdom takes
form in thought and word.

Diagram # 20   The Magical Image of Chokmah

THE HERMETIC QABALAH

Chapter 20

The Beginning

Kether, the first Sephirah marks the beginning of positive existence. What is positive existence? Simply, it is all that has taken place since the beginning. If that sounds like we are talking in circles, perhaps that is because when discussing the beginning of existence, it is often necessary. Using a finite instrument like human consciousness to explain or understand an infinite subject, such as eternity, has its problems.

It might be useful to consider an evolutionary concept contained in the Vedas. According to the teachings of this ancient text, Brahma is said to have created the world with one out-breath. Later it is destroyed by the in-breath of Shiva. According to this teaching, existence has always alternated between cycles of expanding manifestation followed by those which contract. In other words, the Universe is breathed forth and then returns to its source. Hence, we may use the analogy of

THE HERMETIC QABALAH

in and out breathing. This has a parallel in the Qabalah with its "Lightning Flash" of primary manifestation followed by the return to Kether, symbolized by the "Serpent of Wisdom." If human consciousness, expresses in repeated cycles of manifestation, then so will God.

But, perhaps more interesting is the fact that modern physicists, with their theory of the Big Bang, seem to affirm these ancient doctrines. Although Physics is still trying to work out a few "kinks" in its theory, Ageless Wisdom perhaps long ago explained these problems and offered solutions. Let's take a look at these explanations.

As we discussed in the Chapter on Qabalah and the Big Bang, there was a "previous ending" before the current beginning. All matter, substance, Cosmic "stuff" existed in one infinitely compact point called the Singularity by physicists and the "Primal or Smooth Point" by the Qabalist. Surrounding it was negative existence—not space, but the potential for space, the Void.

Kether is the point on the paper. Negative existence is the blank sheet of paper on which the point is about to be inscribed.

How was the Primal Point or Singularity created? Well, according to Qabalists, it was the focusing through a swirling activity that drew in negative existence, or all that went before, in a prior cycle of manifestation. This negative existence was said to have three basic characteristics.

THE HERMETIC QABALAH

It was limitless, it had infinite potential, and from it all was derived. Poetically, these characteristics may be expressed as:

AIN, Ain – no-thing (infinite potential);

AIN SUPh, Ain Soph – No-limit – (boundless);

AIN SUPh AUR, Ain Soph Aur – Limitless Light, the basic substance of everything.

This "Limitless Light" spiraled tighter and tighter, driven by the singular force of gravity, into one smooth point. Kether was born.

When the Primal Point reached a critical mass, a great explosion released its energy and positive existence was born. The "Rashith ha-Galgalim" or "The Beginning of the Whirlings" came into being and continues to this day.

That first impulse of the Cosmic Will to create is the root of all subsequent activity, from the manifestation of galaxies to the spin of electrons and beyond. By referencing the principle of the "Law of Response" we know that whatever we are, and whatever we are doing, our Divine victory is assured.

The grade of initiation associated with this Sephirah is "The Ipsissimus." The Ipsissimus is thought to be the most senior of the Magi and, as such, can only be held by one person at a time. This makes sense when taking into consideration that the title is usually translated as, "He who knows himself most." His attainment comes about when, for any life wave, one most closely

THE HERMETIC QABALAH

indentifies his inner Self with the Yekhidah—the indivisible Self of the Cosmic Will.

However, as one of my mentors, Eugene Emard, was fond of pointing out, in every group, there is an Ipsissimus. He would say, "it need not be the most talented or the most educated or the richest. It could, in fact, be a baby!"

The famous Qabalistic aphorism states, "Malkuth is in Kether and Kether is in Malkuth, but after another manner," illustrates an important point. Kether contains the potential of all creation, like a seed. Malkuth is the manifestation of that potential, like the grown, mature tree. The Initiate's role is that of mediator between heaven and earth, because one who has attained this grade of initiation has completely identified with the Primal Will.

In several initiatory schools in the Western Mystery Tradition, considerable time and effort is spent using the imagination to build the Tree in the aura. This theurgical work builds power paths into the fabric of the subtle body of the initiate. These paths act as channels for the transmission of the high tensioned currents of the spiritual energy descending from Kether. This is the experience of the grace of God.

Kether in Hebrew literally means "The Crown." It is connected to the uppermost chakra or inner holy planet known in the East as the "Thousand Petal Lotus." This is the organ of spiritual vision referred to in the West as the Mercury Center. When fully awakened by the serpent power, it appears in the aura as a crown of light

THE HERMETIC QABALAH

resting just above the head. This chakra receives the spiritual energy from the higher planes and triggers the confection of the stone within the pineal gland. When this occurs all of the inner sensorium vibrates together in a balanced and harmonious manner. This experience leads to perfect health and the extension of the life span far beyond what is normally possible.

This awakening of the Mercury center is mentioned in scripture as the "single eye." "If Thy eye be single, your body will be filled with light."[*Matthew* 6:22] This light provides the illumination associated with, for example, Paul on the road to Damascus. It is this energy that is described as the "Powder of Projection" in alchemy. When the energy is projected onto others by a Master of Wisdom, it may in turn, trigger illumination in those persons upon which it is projected. This act is known as initiation by impartation.

As this energy increases, the Master must likewise increase his giving. This is a fundamental law. We must always project the Hidden Light of the One Life in order to make room for more.

In the Minor Arcana of the Tarot, Kether is represented by the four aces. Note that in each of these cards, the relevant implement is held in a hand emerging from a cloud. This refers to the fact that spiritual truth as represented by Kether, is not based on anything outside of itself, but is self-sustaining. This Truth is absolute and is not relative. Kether represents the ALL, from which nothing can be taken away and to which nothing

THE HERMETIC QABALAH

can be added. It is an ever evolving, transformative perfection.

The colors for Kether's image are: Brilliance; Pure White Brilliance; White flecked with Gold.

THE HERMETIC QABALAH

I am the center of expression for the
Primal-Will-to Good, which eternally
creates and sustains the universe.

Diagram #21   The Magical Image of Kether

THE HERMETIC QABALAH

Part V

The Serpent of Wisdom

(Paths on the Tree of Life)

THE HERMETIC QABALAH

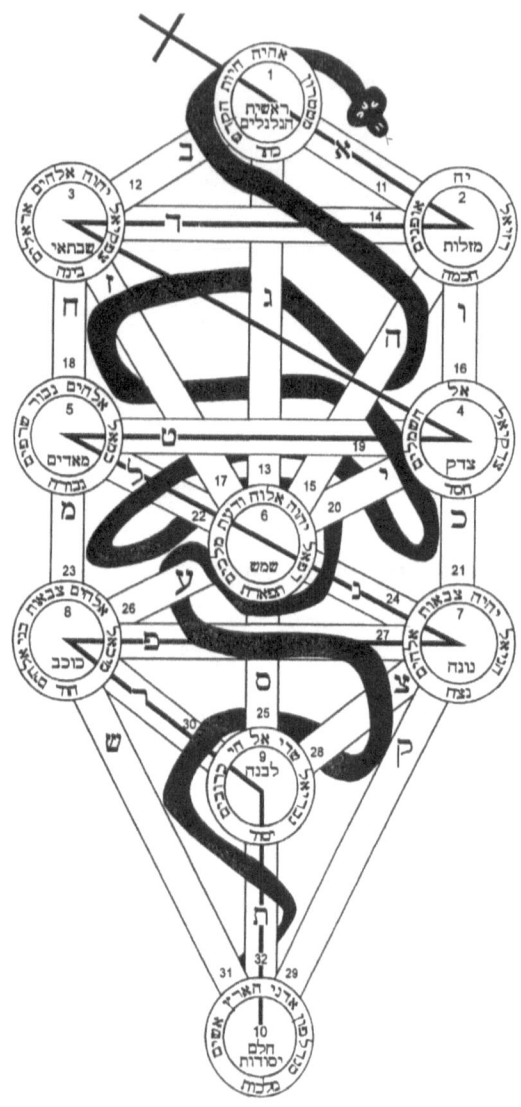

Diagram #22   The Serpent of Wisdom on the Tree of Life

THE HERMETIC QABALAH

Chapter 21
The Serpent of Wisdom

"The Serpent of wisdom crosses each of the twenty-two paths but never enters any of the Sephiroth. Note its color is black, sometimes assigned to the planet Saturn."
[Theoricus Ritual]

Thus the mechanics of the Golden Dawn system of initiation is summarized. It reveals to us that initiation operates on two levels of consciousness. One, represented by the Sephiroth (which is examined in Part 1), imparts wisdom through objective knowledge. This wisdom is communicated via lectures and diagrams. All knowledge and instruction is transmitted on the receptive level of Briah, which is why the Sephiroth are colored in the "Queen Scale" on the Minutum Mundum diagram of the Tree of Life. In the Golden Dawn Ceremonies, this portion of initiation is assigned to the Sephiroth proper, and to the grades.

Two, the remaining portion of the ceremonies comprise the "approach" to each Sephirah by means of the interconnecting "paths." These rituals include a series of formal, ceremonial "path-workings." In the tradition of the Merkavah School, the candidate is confronted by the guardians of the path. He or she is then allowed to

THE HERMETIC QABALAH

travel or "pass through" only by using arcane passwords and formula.

These paths are represented in the projective, "King Scale" colors of Atziluth on the Minutum Mundum. The King Scale of color attributions keys the deep consciousness into the initiative transforming current. This energy is then grounded through the Queen scale that relates, as we have said to the sephirothic energies.

Hence, the paths taken in reverse order chart a path of spiritual transformation, starting with our physical environment and proceeding, step-by-step, to ultimate union with God. This process is what is known as The Great Work of Initiation.

These paths are represented in the Qabalah by the letters of the Hebrew alphabet. In the Hermetic Qabalistic system, the letters are enriched by the symbols of the Major Arcana of the Tarot.

A cursory examination of this symbol system reveals a paradox. If the Tarot presents the path of initiation, then does the sequence start at the top of the Tree of Life, or at the bottom? All systems following the Western Mysteries, and especially those using the Tree of Life as a blueprint, always start at Malkuth, the physical universe, and trace the way inwardly, ever-deeper, into the worlds of consciousness. When we grasp the tail of the Serpent of Wisdom and follow its winding coils it leads us up the Tree.

THE HERMETIC QABALAH

Conversely, it is the Lightning Flash, symbol of the process of instantaneous creation that descends from Kether at the top of the Tree. Why?

The obvious answer is that the way of transformation, the path of initiation must be established before an aspirant may travel it. Established by whom? God? Perhaps. But this answer is facile. For God is the first and, in the final analysis, is the only actor, the only consciousness there is. What hasn't the Divine established? No, we must look deeper. We must ask ourselves, "If this is the Path of Return, who created this way?" One of the first steps in understanding where we are going is to look at where we have been.

The Western Mystery Tradition teaches that at one time all was "one" with the Godhead. We are now seeking to be reunited with that central presence. God is not static, but dynamic and continually developing. "As above, so below," says the Emerald Tablet. God is an ever evolving perfection. In order to fully enjoy and experience this perfection in creation, God chose to experience it from many different unique perspectives. To that end He/She emanated innumerable parts of the essential unity into seeming separation from the Source (only "seeming" because the Source remains the All). The path leading away from the One is called involution and is represented, on one level, by the Lightning Flash.

But those who seek Initiation must reject a response exhibiting separatism, natural to involution, for it will not succeed. It is anti-evolutionary. For such is the

THE HERMETIC QABALAH

Path of Return, the accelerated, evolutionary journey to union. If this is our choice, we must develop the inner awareness to see the unity behind the appearances of separation. Fortunately, there are tools and techniques to assist. The Arcana of the Tarot provide instructive cues.

The 32nd Path of the Tree of Life is represented, in Tarot, by a dancer. The dancer embodies freedom. Here, she is even dancing on air! But, as any great ballerina, figure skater, or the like will tell us, their art is the product of intense discipline. Discipline involves concentrated restriction.

On the other end of the Tree, we find the 11th Path represented by the Arcanum of The Fool. Here, we see the freedom as an unrestricted Quester out on the open road. However, any student of Tarot symbolism will tell you that the care-free hobo is about to descend into the valley of manifestation, which again implies—restriction. These two states of freedom encompass the entire experience of manifestation and initiation.

Legends in widely different parts of the world and in vastly different cultures state that the Mysteries were taught to man by angels or gods. What is the common origin of these very similar legends? Well, our tradition states that man was not the first of creation to make the journey to individuality and then back again to God. Those who have traveled the path before us are sometimes willing to pause in their progress and turn back to give humankind a helping hand. These "Elder

THE HERMETIC QABALAH

Brothers and Sisters" are called the Manus, or Rishis in the East.

The Logos, (the guiding oversoul of the Solar System whose outer body is the Sun), recruited these advanced souls to guide the development of newly individualized humanity. They, in turn, founded the Mystery Schools in civilizations now long vanished. Although these teachers had long since outgrown the need for physical bodies, they recognized that the beginning instruction of humankind would have to be accomplished on the physical plane. These advanced beings would form bodies, not using the normal channel of birth, but by successively lowering their vibratory rate until a quasi-physical vehicle would be formed around their etheric matrix. They would hold this form until the instruction was completed and then let their vibration revert to its normal, non-physically visible rate. This procedure is the reason for numerous accounts of miraculous appearances of "angels" and "gods."

These Manus gathered around themselves the most promising of the then primitive humans, and impressed by means of a telepathic process, instructional images. Language was in its infancy at this time and was poorly equipped to impart the intricacies of the teachings. Even today, subconsciousness responds rather poorly to mere language labels, however cleverly phrased. Much greater results are obtained by using sensory images, color and visual symbols, as well as chants and mantras. This is especially true of ritual and

THE HERMETIC QABALAH

ceremonial, which can blend all of these, and may be blended into one multifaceted Arcanum.

The suggestions planted in the deep consciousness of the aspirant have energy of their own. They germinate and attract their macrocosmic counterpart in the larger world and alter the conscious perception of the aspirant. Eventually, they flower forth into full-blown realizations, transforming the personality and the physical body of the Initiate.

In the following chapters, we will examine the interconnecting paths symbolized by the letters of the Hebrew alphabet and their corresponding Tarot Arcana to gain insight into the initiatory process. It is the energy of these paths that stimulates, awakens, and balances the inner powers of the soul. This process transforms the humble seeker into a fully realized Adept.

THE HERMETIC QABALAH

Chapter 22
The 32nd *Path of the Letter Tav*
The Administrative Intelligence

The first path in our journey of awakening is that of the 32nd, symbolized by the Hebrew letter Tav, the 21st Arcanum of the Tarot, named "The World," and the planetary attribution of Saturn.

It is associated in the Qabalistic classic, *The 32 Paths of Wisdom,* with the title, "The Administrative Intelligence." This path is also designated as, "The Serving Intelligence," as the desire to serve permeates all true Mystery Schools at all levels, from the humble Neophyte to that of the highest Magus. It is this key quality that opens the door of the Temples of Initiation. It is, indeed, the only safe and effective motive for traveling the ancient Path of Return.

At first, the Aspirant, while she may have the desire to serve, usually lacks the skills and abilities, The old Zen phrase, "chop wood and carry water," describes her fitness. Thus, the new initiate serves in whatever capacity she can in order to pay for her training. While in a true school of initiation no charge is ever *required*

THE HERMETIC QABALAH

for teaching, there are still expenses. In other words, the sincere aspirant is never turned away because of the inability to pay. However, it is a test of the candidate's sincerity and suitability that they voluntarily offer whatever payment they can. This payment is usually made through time, treasure, or talent. It has long been observed that it is part of human nature that that which is gotten easily or for free is valued little. It is also a violation of universal law.

But there is another aspect of service that is rarely touched on. It is this. Quite simply the more advanced lessons cannot be learned except though service to others, to the tradition, or to God. Only when the aspirant shifts from the motivation of "getting" to "giving," will the doors of the higher mysteries open.

Tarot Arcanum #21, "The World," is assigned to the seventh and final stage of Spiritual Unfoldment, which is known as Cosmic Consciousness. As it is service that admits us to the temple, it is also service that paves the way to the realization of the oneness of the universe. As Jesus said, "Let he who will be chief become as a servant."

As previously mentioned, the planet Saturn is attributed to this path. Astrologically, Saturn is related to the energy of limitation, discipline, and form. It is through these expressions of the Saturn energy that the aspirant conceives and refines his goal. This goal setting activity galvanizes the energy and power of the deep consciousness which brings the connections, resources, skills, and realizations that are used to perfect the transformation into "Homo-Adeptus." Until we understand this power of limitation we will not be able to achieve liberation.

Examine the central figure in *The World*. She (or He/She since the figure is really a hermaphrodite) is a dancer. She is the epitome of grace and freedom. But, as anyone who has worked in ballet or a chorus line will tell you, countless hours of stretching, bar work, and practice goes into the preparation of the performance. The same may be said of martial arts. Spins and kicks

THE HERMETIC QABALAH

are practiced hundreds and thousands of times until muscle memory takes over and the moves are made with refinement and finesse. Proficiency and freedom require discipline, limitation, and focus. The power that limits is the key to liberation.

In the *Sepher Yetzirah* each one of the Hebrew double letters (those having two pronunciations) is assigned a planetary attribution and a pair of opposites. These pairs are known in the Western Tradition as the "contraries." For example, the letter Tav, assigned to this 32nd Path is assigned to the contraries, *Dominion and Slavery*. It is through the exercise of the limiting Saturn force that we may choose to achieve dominion (i.e. Mastery) over the slavery to our challenges.

The 32nd path is the first path leading to the inner, spiritual worlds. These worlds are depicted by the rest of the Tree, which, in scripture, is stated to be planted in the East of the Garden of Eden. In the story of The Fall, in the book of Genesis, we read that God placed the Kerubim at the gate of the garden to guard the way of the Tree of Life. These guardian angels are represented by the four holy creatures in the corners of the 21st Arcanum of the Tarot. Here, we see the Lion, Eagle, Man, and Ox. It is said that they wield a flaming sword to guard the way. Another name for the Lightning Flash is *The Flaming Sword*.

Accordingly, when symbolically walking the 32nd path we are reentering the Garden of Eden.

THE HERMETIC QABALAH

The central figure in Key #21, holds two vortices of energy, one in each hand. One represents the destructive, tearing down energy. In the other hand she holds the constructive or "building up" current. Thus is depicted the "solve et coagula" of the alchemists. Dissolve and reform, when channeled in perfect equilibrium, holds the secret of the Great Work—the regeneration of consciousness.

This path links our perceptions of the manifest world to its matrix found in our deep consciousness. This inner consciousness is the realm of the Collective Unconscious, to use the Jungian term. Here is the so-called Akashic Library, the record of all experience and thought. The home of all symbols. This level contains all of the spiritual realizations of the ancient sages. But it also holds the patterns of past errors. As said before, discrimination is the first virtue of the Path.

This need for discriminative judgment requires the advancing initiate to test each perception and reaction. It necessitates honesty and a complete self-assessment. Only then can we safely investigate the fantasies of the astral world represented by Yesod.

At this level the elemental and astral consciousness interact with our personal mental patterns and become the templates on which we create our physical reality. These are the "keys to the Kingdom."

We must exercise a penetrating gaze, separating illusion from truth in order to pursue the path of

THE HERMETIC QABALAH

transformation. This discrimination is gained by the systematic acquisition of knowledge.

The Hebrew title of the grade associated with Yesod is *Baal ha-Daath* or Master of Knowledge. As the old saying goes:

> "How do you gain Wisdom?"
> "By making right choices."
> "How do you learn to make right choices?"
> "By making wrong choices."

The wreath surrounding the dancer in this 21st key symbolizes the acquisition of knowledge through experience. Its individual leaves have been woven by human learning and skill. The shape of the wreath is that of the cosmic egg or the "zero," both which are symbolic of the alpha and the omega.

It is through the organized study of our own responses that we build constructive habit patterns, the basis of our new reality. But it cannot be accomplished using the intellect alone. As the Master "R" once said, "The intellect is a dull can opener with which to probe the secrets of the heart." We must practice the Hierogamos or divine mating of our mind with our heart to conceive and give birth to our illuminated state of consciousness.

At this stage on the path it is important to acknowledge our inner powers of consciousness, if only in principle. True, at this point we have plenty to learn in gaining

THE HERMETIC QABALAH

skill to use them effectively; but that facility will come with practice.

If we strive to shift our identity from our imperfect work-in-progress personality to the Individuality that is our inner, essential self, we will truly learn the meaning of service and will dance in perfect rhythm the steps of the cosmic dance.

The planet Saturn is associated with what in the Eastern Tradition is called the Kundalini or serpent fire. This transforming, sacred, nerve energy is the power that transforms the physical into the mystical solar body of the Adepts. It is the residual, sexual energy stored at the sacral center at the base of the spine. During a series of exercises relating to the unwritten Qabalah, this energy is stirred into activity and is directed sequentially upwards along the subtle channels of the spinal canal. This awakens the other inner holy planets, metals, or chakras into a fully functioning state.

It has been emphasized repeatedly in the writings of the tradition that this awakening should not be forced or performed prematurely. Either can lead to serious physical and mental health problems.

This is because the chakras, known also as the inner holy planets or the inner sacred metals in the alchemical writings of the West, act as energy exchangers on the subtle levels of consciousness. Like their physical organ counterparts, the nerve complexes

THE HERMETIC QABALAH

and endocrine glands associated with them, each play an important role in the overall health of the individual. If these centers are activated while in an unbalanced state, the imbalance becomes exacerbated and can trigger a release of certain hormones that can produce aberrant perception and behavior.

Often the ego is the primary motivation for forcing the rise of the kundalini. The desire to acquire and exercise power is based on the fear of inadequacy and the lie of separation.

On the other hand, the motivation to serve is the highest demonstration of power and is based on the reality of Oneness. This leads to a balanced development. As Hermes said,

"Equilibrium is the secret of the Great Work."

THE HERMETIC QABALAH

Chapter 23
The 31st Path of the Letter Shin, "The Perpetual Intelligence"

The 31st path is the holy path of mystical fire. This is because it is attributed to the Hebrew letter Shin which corresponds to the element of fire. On the Cube of Space (page 141) it is assigned to the coordinate that connects the North (symbolizing the future) to the South (which represents the past). It is the energy of universal fire that is constantly transforming each moment of manifestation to the next in the drama of creation. It is the string upon which the beads of manifestation are connected.

The numerical value of the letter Shin is 300. This is a very important attribution in the Literal Qabalah for 300 is the value of the phrase, "Ruach Elohim," or Spirit of God (i.e. The Holy Spirit). Hence, in ceremonial the fire is always a symbol for the divine power which transforms and regenerates. This is the real identity of everything and of every living creature.

In the *32 Paths of Wisdom*, Shin is called Saykel Temidiy or the Perpetual or Eternal Intelligence. Paul Case connects this power to our identification of self with the ONE SELF, the certain knowing of

THE HERMETIC QABALAH

immortality. This is the fruit of the Tree of Life—conscious immortality—and the hallmark of a realized Adept.

Yet, the seed of this experience is planted in the initiate relatively early on the Path of Return. Ceremonially this is conferred as the aspirant travels the path connecting Malkuth to the sphere of the intellect, Hod. Here, an intellectual comprehension of immortality is begun. Later, this seed will flower into a full realization in the Greater Mysteries. Now, it is enough to meditate on the facts revealed by modern physics. That is, that the essence of all forms is eternal, is continual, and is one. This essence is named by the Sages as the Secret Fire. It is an energy that constitutes all material form. It is the energy that propels the galaxies into motion. It is the energy which holds all on their course. In everything we do, experience, or create the working of this all-encompassing dance of the alternating effects of the universal fire is found.

The 31st Path is assigned to the Hebrew Mother letter, assigned in the *Sepher Yetzirah* to the element of fire. Fire as we have pointed out is the "transforming" element. As we have said, it is through the sacred, secret fire that an initiate is transformed into an Adept. Through its action, specialized in the Kundalini, the inner holy planets or metals are awakened and aroused into full activity.

THE HERMETIC QABALAH

This act is symbolized by the sound waves emerging from the Angel's trumpet in the Tarot Arcanum assigned to this path. This heightening of vibration increases the intensity of all our inner activity. This is the fire that purges the dross to reveal the true gold of the alchemists. It dissolves the old patterns of error to reform the personality into a more perfect image of the Perpetual Intelligence. Once this energy is liberated, it becomes responsive to the new patterns impressed on it by the Higher Self. These new perceptions, awakened by the Higher Self, are represented by the three figures rising out of the coffins of limited three-dimensional sense experience.

THE HERMETIC QABALAH

This awakening process is fraught with many hazards and the symbolic design of Key #20 illustrates the correct (and safe) procedure for awakening.

The man and woman represent the individual aspirant's self and subconscious respectively. Their coffins symbolize the limited sense experience from which they are emerging. The Higher self, symbolized by the archangel, responds to their upward yearning by blowing his elongated trumpet.

The child represents the awakening, balanced personality. He is aspiring, reaching to embrace the Higher Self.

By their posture we see that subconsciousness has been purified of the negative patterns of immature expressions of consciousness. Self-consciousness has become a passive witness to the work of L.V.X., the Hidden Light.

This shift of identification from the Personality to the Higher Self is a major transition that must occur before the Fire can be safely raised to complete the Philosopher's Stone in the Mercury Center of the forebrain.

This Higher Self is seen here personified as the archangel Gabriel, "the strength of God." Gabriel is the archangel of Water. This dual emphasis of Water and Fire holds a great secret in the alchemical process. Water, symbolic of mind, is the vehicle of Fire, the symbol of spirit. Our desire and aspiration opens our inner senses so that we may become vehicles of the Perpetual Intelligence.

THE HERMETIC QABALAH

Chapter 24
The 30th Path of the Letter Resh
The Collective Intelligence

The 30th Path connects the Sephiroth Yesod with Hod, or, the sphere of the subconscious mind with that of the intellect.

The intellect has the power to select any image from the library of the Collective Consciousness, and to hold that image steady by employing concentration. This selected image may then be energized by the desire force, to become a matrix for manifestation.

This 30th path holds the key to this interactive process.

Attributed to this Path is the Hebrew letter Resh (meaning face) and its Tarot Arcanum, the Sun.

THE HERMETIC QABALAH

Here we see a young boy and girl representing our regenerated self and subconsciousness. This process of awakening, or the completing and balancing of our personality, is performed by our Individuality or Higher Self symbolized by the solar disk in this Tarot design.

When a young child draws a picture of the sun, he or she will most often draw a face on it. This "happy face" is an intuitive expression of the realization that the physical sun is the body of a vast consciousness known as the Solar Logos. Its consciousness is similar to our Individuality but much vaster in degree.

In recognition of this fact, initiates often use the phrase, "Light in extension."

THE HERMETIC QABALAH

As mentioned previously, the 30th Path ascends from Yesod or the Collective Unconsciousness, to Hod, the intellect. In one sense, this connection symbolizes the acquisition of knowledge necessary for the initiate to transform the misconceptions of the Great Lies into a new understanding of Truth. The Lies of Separation, Mortality, and Materialism must be dissolved. Their effects must be replaced by a firm understanding of the truths of Unity, Immortality, and Spirit.

The young children in this Tarot design represent the emerging birth of a new consciousness. Up to this point, Nature has evolved the human body and consciousness to that of *Homo sapiens*. The Divine, acting in concert with the self-consciousness of humanity, must now give birth to the next step—*Homo Illuminatus*.

This transformation or rebirth is known as the "Operation of the Sun." No longer do we identify with the shifting sands of our personality. Rather, we know ourselves to be the rock of the Individuality, the one ego seated in our hearts.

This is the realization that we are striving to make definite. We do this using the practicing concentration of Hod. This discipline is necessary to elaborate and establish those patterns that help form the theory residing in Yesod.

The more consistently we elaborate and activate these patterns of truth in our daily routine, the more rapidly we prepare ourselves for the shift of identity. This is the role of the *Practicus*. It requires consistent and regular practice and is symbolized by the dance of the children inside the magic circle of the fairy ring. This realization is further depicted by the budding sunflower.

THE HERMETIC QABALAH

When we undertake this practice, we must apply all of our powers of observation, imagination, and intellect to build a new matrix of conscious and unconscious patterns. We must align ourselves with the solar energy, symbolized by the thirteen Yods falling from the sun. Thirteen is the number of Unity, Love, and the Void and these three words are the "keys" to the regenerative process.

It is through our attention that we lift our hearts and realize the link between our Individuality, the Higher Self, and our Personality. We must come to love our true Self, just as a child loves and trusts his parents. We must become "as a little child."

The Hebrew titles of the two grades of initiation associated with Yesod and Hod provide a clue to the activity of this stage. Yesod is called Baal ha-Daath which translates as Master of Knowledge. Hod's title is Baal ha-Omen, a Master of Truth or Verity. Daath relates to knowledge obtained through direct perception, sometimes called Gnosis. It also carries the related meaning of Union and refers to Union with the Higher Self. This direct perception based on contact with the Higher Self reveals the "Truth" that lies at the center of all existence.

THE HERMETIC QABALAH

Chapter 25
The 29th Path of the Letter Qoph
The Corporeal Intelligence

THE HERMETIC QABALAH

Every clear, emotionally energized, mental image tends to find expression in the material world as an actual condition or event.

Spirit and matter are the poles of a continuum known as consciousness. There is no "mind over matter," for matter is a manifestation of mind—of consciousness. Spirit is not an antagonistic opponent of the manifested world. Instead, they are different vibrations of the same essential substance known as mind.

The first path on the approach to the Sephirah Netzach, the sphere of desire, is attributed the Corporeal (or Bodily) Intelligence. This path connects the middle pillar of consciousness to the right-hand pillar of force. It is through the conjunction of matter and the desire force that all physical transformation occurs. Thus, this connection is not energized until the advancing initiate has learned to exert some control over the intellect as demonstrated in the preceding grade of Practicus and its Sephirah, Hod.

One of the keys to this control is the ability to recognize and work with cycles. We see this highlighted in the Tarot Arcanum "The Moon," assigned to this path. The Moon tides are some of the best examples we have of cycles. The regular, monthly waxing; full; waning; and dark phases have been connected in our consciousness with the tides of the ocean, crimes of passion, and menstruation. Ritualists, especially the practitioners of lunar formula magic, such as our Wiccan Brothers and Sisters, will attempt to coordinate their work with these tides. They initiate operations of invocation and manifestation during the cycle of the waxing moon, while banishment and elimination works are performed at the beginning of the waning cycle.

THE HERMETIC QABALAH

In every effective endeavor, there must be periods of rest and reflection balancing the active times of advancement and striving. This is symbolized in the Tarot design by the rolling hills and the yellow royal path.

The Path of Qoph connects the grades of Zelator, attributed to Malkuth, to that of Philosophus, assigned to Netzach. This path therefore combines the qualities of zeal and desire. For most people desire is a different, sometimes tempestuous force that might be compared to the ocean crashing on the beach. But for the initiate, the practices of Theoricus and especially Practicus have developed the discipline and skill needed to direct this dynamic power. This "focusing" of power might be comparable to directing the flow of the surf through a turbine, to produce electricity.

The zodiacal sign assigned to this path is Pisces, well known for its devotional quality. No matter how skilled we may become at holding an imaginational form in our mind, only this quality of "devotion" can unleash the mystical power of our desire force needed to give birth to our endeavor.

It is the caring devotional charge of our desire force, directed with aspirational fervor towards the expression of our Higher Self, which completes the transmutation process. This strong, dynamic force imprints the individual consciousness and its trillions of physical cells to generate a pattern for our new creation. [Readers are directed to Dr. Lloyd Benson's ground breaking book *The Biology of Belief*, for further information on this].

An examination of the symbols that make up the 18th Arcanum, reveal a basis in the ancient Qabalistic

THE HERMETIC QABALAH

aphorism, "First the Stone, then the Plant, then the Animal, then the Man, and then more than Man." This recognition of the process of evolution emphasizes the continuous development of the Divine Consciousness throughout the process of creation. Nature's achievement of the miracle of human consciousness is the foundation or springboard for the adaptive transformative process that leads to Adeptship.

In the Qabalah, the letter Qoph is attributed to the function of sleep. It is during sleep that the new patterns are incorporated into our cells. It is also during this period, when our conscious minds and their Beta brain waves are in abeyance, that healing and repair take place.

The name of the letter, Qoph, means "Back of the head." This is the location of the Medulla Obbligato, the Pons and the other section of the brain that govern the functions that regulate, heal, and modify our body. It is this location that is the interface between the so-called higher functions of the conscious mind and the subconscious activities. Imprints made on these cells by the imagination flow to the consciousness of the cells in the rest of the body.

This is also the seat of the subtle hearing (clairaudient) faculty that connects the meditative personality to the Akashic Records, the memory of nature. As our personal memory is really a specialization of this more universal level, all recoveries from the Akashic library are, in fact, an activity of remembering. The "bringing through" of these impressions in a large part is based on our skills in recollection. For this reason, in past ages great emphasis was placed by the esoteric schools on the art of memory. Renaissance adepts like Bruno would develop elaborate systems of mnemonics that are still in

THE HERMETIC QABALAH

use today. The Tarot, in one application, is an example of this. In periods when the ecclesiastical authorities would torture and put to death anyone found with written texts dealing with the arcane subjects, important doctrines were transmitted orally and preserved in the memory of initiates. Even today, members of the Order of Freemasonry routinely memorize pages and pages of ritual and lecture. They then deliver it word perfect on a regular basis.

This skill enhances the ability of the initiate to access the inner levels of instruction that imprints the cellular consciousness of their vehicles, altering and subtly transforming themselves into a new being.

Qoph, through its connections with Pisces relates to the beginning of development of psychic awareness. This is not the untrained, natural psychism of which many Neophytes are so proud. In fact, that type of gift is more often than not, a hindrance to inner development. No, in this system of training, the regular, disciplined, systematic awakening of the subtle senses is undertaken. In this way, the gifts are more efficient and serviceable and will produce much higher results than those manifested outside the esoteric schools.

A subject that is often raised by students involves the use of consciousness-altering drugs as an adjunct to mystical work. It is absolutely true that alterations of the chemistry of the blood and the central nervous system can mimic mystical states of awareness similar to illumination. Richard Alpert became Ram Dass after experimenting with psychotropics. It has even been suggested that Siddhartha Gautama became the Buddha after eating figs growing from the Bodhi Tree, a variety named Ficcus Religiosa which is known to promote the manufacture of serotonin.

THE HERMETIC QABALAH

We must consider that the drug induced opening of the subtle gates of perception, is in some cases effective. But are we prepared for what may be revealed on the other side? Has the experimenter developed the discipline and control to deal with the visions? Has his philosophical understanding of the laws of consciousness evolved to the point that he can direct those forces contacted? Has he developed the skills needed to avoid damaging the delicate balance of the subtle sensorium? Can he close the gates in order to be able to function in daily life?

The trained subconsciousness of an initiate *can* deal with the fine adjustments of the chemistry of a naturally induced illumination experience. The drug initiated experimenter is using something equivalent to a sledge hammer to batter down the gates of the inner sensorium. There will be those who insist that they know better than the sages and will persist in employing drugs in search of the fast path or shortcut to awakening. I can only say, "Good luck." I hope you are the exception rather than the rule. It will be an interesting trip, I'm sure!"

"I desire to know in order to serve," is the key that opens the door of the Mysteries. This deep, devotion to serve the Light, Humanity, and the Higher Self must be the primary motive if the candidate is to tread the path of illumination safely and successfully. Until the aspirant has shifted from the seeker to the server, until he or she has shifted from a perspective of "what can I get" to "what may I give" no real or significant progress will be made.

THE HERMETIC QABALAH

Chapter 26
The 23rd Path of the Letter Tzaddi
The Natural Intelligence

The 23rd Path ascends from the Sephirah Yesod, attributed to the grade of Theoricus and terminates in the Sephirah Netzach, with the grade of Philosophus. The zodiacal attribution is the sign Aquarius. The Tarot attribution is Key #17, The Star.

Dissolution is the alchemical stage assigned to this path. It is perhaps one of the hardest stages for an Aspirant to work through, for it concerns the concept of the Personality. Normally people identify, "self" with the personality, even with all of its foibles, insecurities, and instabilities.

This complex is made up of habits, emotions, and prejudices that many times are simply expressions of the shifting sands of the Collective Unconsciousness' misinterpretations of experience. These Lies are then reflected into the process manifesting as daily life. No wonder so many lives are chaotic. The matrix of identification has as its foundation the shifting sands of reaction!

The truth is that we are not our ever-changing personality. The power of the Self does not originate from within, but instead flows through it from a higher, more permanent source we call the Individuality. This

THE HERMETIC QABALAH

force, held in focus by our interior stars (chakras) gives the illusion of separation so necessary for incarnation and dealing with time and space. The trouble arises when we mistake this illusion for a reality that doesn't exist.

This is the great truth that is revealed, not by words, but by looking within, as in deep meditation. Meditation, if properly practiced, will have the effect of balancing and synchronizing the activity of the inner holy centers. This "synching" brings the realization that the individual aspirant is a participant in the great cosmic flow of consciousness and creation. This realization, far beyond being a mere intellectual concept, becomes a quantum change a paradigm shift on which all the higher realizations are based.

To accomplish this, we must to surrender out-worn concepts, even those that are cherished. By surrendering, we create the space and freedom needed to embrace new and more sublime illuminations.

This shift allows the initiate to embody the universal principles she is striving to comprehend. The illusion that any of our preconceptions, be they expressed as ideas, thoughts, or emotions, originate within us, is stripped away. We instead embrace the idea that the consciousness flowing through us is Cosmic in origin.

This is the revelation of Truth that is discovered during the act of meditation. We are freed from the bondage of the lies in the Collective Unconsciousness of Yesod, and our consciousness is tuned to the truths shining down from our true self in Tiphareth.

The symbol of the Green Cube is also associated with this path. Green is the secondary color derived from a

THE HERMETIC QABALAH

balanced blend of the primary colors Blue and Yellow. This reveals some interesting concepts. Alchemically, yellow relates to principle of Mercury, that which flows and transforms and is the Ray of Wisdom. Blue, on the other hand, deals with the alchemical principle of Salt, which has the qualities of stability and preservation and the Ray of Love. A perfect balance of these two principles relates to the balance or equilibrium which is said to be the secret of the Great Work.

The goal of this great work is the recognition and embodiment of truth that is symbolized by the cube itself. This geometric solid has always been a symbol of ultimate truth. This is because no matter which of its sides serves as its base, it remains the same. In other words, from whatever point of view you examine the cube it is always constant and agrees with itself. Further, each cube has 8 corners, 12 edges, and 6 sides (See Diagram #17 The Cube of Space on page 141). Thus the number that defines any cube is 26. This is a special number in Qabalah because it is the number of the Tetragrammaton or sacred, ineffable name of God, (IHVH). IHVH symbolizes the divine essential reality at the core of all existence. In the Qabalistic Cube of Space the center is assigned, in the Sepher Yetzirah, to the Creator. If we close our eyes and meditate on the location with this cube we invariably find that it coincides with ourselves. Here is the closest we can come to putting the Great Truth into words. This is the truth that is revealed in meditation.

THE HERMETIC QABALAH

Students are sometimes uncertain about what is actually meant in the Hermetic Qabalah in reference to meditation. They confuse meditation with other usually Eastern systems. Many times this is because the languages of the West have no words to adequately designate what has been translated as meditation. Thus terms like Zen "Zazen" became "Zen Meditation." Mantric exercises are similarly confused.

Meditation in the Western sense is an active, intense activity. It is not just sitting and attempting to blank the mind, or concentrating on the breath. True, it does require relaxation, breathing, and concentration; but, it also requires an intention—a defined purpose. It concerns the deliberate use of the Law of Suggestion to probe deeper into the personal subconsciousness until a break though is made into the intuitional levels of the Individuality.

THE HERMETIC QABALAH

In the Tarot Key assigned to this path, The Star, the Ibis bird sacred to Mercury, is at rest in the tree, indicating that the activity of meditation requires the quiescence of the intellect. The main figure of the key, a young nude woman, represents our consciousness when it is balanced perfectly between the land and water, indicating the balance necessary between awareness of the outer and the inner world, known as the "waking state," designated by Alpha brain activity. We all pass through this state every night and morning when going to sleep or awakening. This is the same territory treaded by true meditation. We must learn to balance and prolong our experience in order to effectively meditate.

The zodiacal sign of Aquarius is assigned to this path. In the Qabalah, this sign is attributed to the tribe of Israel MNShH, *Manaseh*. This name in Gematria, equals 395. This is also the number of H-ShMIM, *Ha-Shamayim*, "The heavens." This title is assigned to the second Sephirah, Chokmah on the Tree of Life and to the life energy known in the Qabalah as ChI or *Chai*. When we meditate correctly we open ourselves up to become channels for the expression for this power. Our vehicles become conduits for the expression of the Life Energy. This has the effect, as pointed out earlier, of harmonizing our inner holy planets, symbolized by the smaller stars in the Tarot picture, with the universal Chai represented by the large eight-pointed star.

This alignment, if done regularly and in coordination with the other practices of inner alchemy, results in the proper raising of the Serpent of Wisdom which activates our inner sensorium.

THE HERMETIC QABALAH

Chapter 27
The 27th Path of the letter Peh
The Exciting Intelligence

The 27th path is the lowest of the three *Reciprocal Paths*, those connecting the Pillar of Mercy to the Pillar of Severity. All three of these paths are connected to the functioning of the Mars Force. This force manifests on the physical plane as the sex drive, but it also has many different functions. It is not surprising, therefore, to find this path assigned to the letter Peh, the planet Mars and the sixteenth Arcanum of the Tarot, called *The Tower*.

THE HERMETIC QABALAH

This path is also the last path traveled in the approach to the 4=7 grade of Philosophus. It is assigned to the second stage of spiritual unfoldment named *Awakening* or *Illumination*.

What if everything you have ever known or believed in was wrong? Could you embrace the new knowledge, the new truths? Or would you instead cling to the comfortable illusions you have treasured in the past? Ignorance is bliss, they say. Well "they" are wrong! Ignorance is slavery and bondage.

Change can be uncomfortable and is often scary. It requires courage and the will to confront. Courage and Will are Martian qualities. They are not, however, personal qualities. They originate with the original creative impulse of the Cosmos. Contrary to popular theology, we do not possess free will. For, there is only one will—the will of the Divine. What we possess personally is the freedom of choice. We can choose to align with the cosmic impulse or to battle it.

On the Cube of Space, the diagonal connecting the North-East edge with the South-West edge is assigned to the letter Peh final. This letter represents the exalted functioning of the Mars force. The South-West edge is assigned to the zodiacal sign Scorpio, the so-called "night house of Mars." On the human body, this sign is attributed to the area of the genitals. The etheric vehicle contains the Mars chakra in this same area. These organs express the energy of reproduction and sexual expression.

The North-East corner of the Cube is attributed to the sign Aries—the day house of Mars. The part of the body corresponding to this sign is the frontal lobe of the brain

THE HERMETIC QABALAH

and the pineal (or Mercury) Chakra. This is the organ of spiritual vision.

This series of symbolic attributions reveals an important process in alchemy. The "raising" of the Mars force (also called the Serpent Fire) from the area of the physical, reproductive expression, to the "higher" organ of spiritual vision, results in an awakening.

This, as the picture of The Tower suggests, can be a traumatic experience. Remember Saint Paul's awakening on the road to Damascus as portrayed in the book of Acts. Here, he was struck temporarily blind. Now this is an extreme example but suggests that this is a difficult path to tread. We can however prepare our consciousness for the experience by identifying with our true Self and becoming receptive to change.

The crown being toppled in the Tarot design is the symbol of our false ego, based on the acceptance of the Lie of Separation, symbolized by the isolated pinnacle on which the tower stands.

The tower itself is a fort or castle, built for defensive purposes on an inaccessible peak. The Lie of Separation is based on the fallacy that there is someone, or something, to defend against. At the root of this delusion is fear. When not balanced, fear is a harmful and destructive emotion. Fear is the basis of aggression, hate, xenophobia, and violence. As the old Taoist saying puts it, "If we are without fear, the Tiger will find no place to put its claws." The greatest basis for a firm self-defense is the courageous absence of fear. Fear, or rather giving in to fear, is failure, for it inhibits action. It robs the heart of strength and propels the coward into self-destruction.

THE HERMETIC QABALAH

Yet, separation and fear are based on an illusion, symbolized by the fact that the Tower is constructed of bricks instead of stone. This represents the artificial construct of the intellect. The problem arises because the intellect is not created to deal with the realities of the spiritual life. It is merely an instrument of the True Self.

This idea is further emphasized by the symbolic detail of the 22 courses of masonry. These represent the elements of written or spoken language. Language is sourced in shared experience. Two people must have a common understanding of phenomena in order to communicate via language. Trying to describe a thunderstorm to, for example, an ancient desert dweller of Egypt, who had never witnessed this event, would be difficult. In fact, in an ancient papyrus it was described as "the Nile flowing sideways in the sky!" So, it makes sense that to rely on written or spoken words to describe a spiritual, nonphysical experience would be fraught with difficulties.

Yet, the false ego, usurping the throne of the Self, attempts to do just that. Its misconception of reality is destined to Fall. This flash of awakening is represented by the lightning strike from the sun. The source of this destruction is the bold, but loving action of our true Self, dissolving our errors so that we may formulate conceptions closer to truth.

This is not comfortable. Change is inherently so. It has even been said, "Better a devil we know than one we don't."

Our long held beliefs, habits, thought patterns, and actions have to be re-evaluated. We cannot become illumined if we remain unchanged. As long as we base

THE HERMETIC QABALAH

our self-identity and our worth on these outward standards, our house is built on illusion. The Universe and the True Self will prune our awareness and ready it for growth.

We must cultivate the skill to look at ourselves objectively, critically assessing our motivations, our strengths and weaknesses, uncolored by the fears of inadequacy and insecurity. We must uphold the highest standard of self-honesty and dedicate ourselves to transformation into the new image of the highest.

Yet we need not do this alone. We may, trustingly accept the guidance of our Individuality, our higher and true Self, who will lovingly perform the transformation.

The stage of unfoldment assigned to this path is called Awakening. This is a very real conscious experience. It is the outcome of all the soul's searching, contemplation, and reflection. It is a vision of the higher reality of the Truth of the Cosmic.

THE HERMETIC QABALAH

Chapter 28
The 26th Path of the Letter Ayin
The Renewing Intelligence & the Power of Humor

This path is assigned to the channel connecting Tiphareth to Hod, the sphere of the Higher Self to the sphere of the Intellect.

This path, via its connection with Key #15 the Devil, is attributed to the first stage of spiritual unfoldment. This stage is referred to as Bondage. This fact sometimes confuses the beginning student because bondage and limitation are almost universally viewed as bad, something to be overcome. Adepts view it quite differently. They know that no manifestation is possible without limitation. All expressions of creation are a focusing of choices with each choice eliminating other avenues of expression. This limiting of possibilities then paves the way for the manifestation of the desired form in the world of time and space. The Adept then functions as the cause, not the effect.

THE HERMETIC QABALAH

The Lie of Materialism is represented in the Tarot Arcanum by the horned male figure standing chained, in front of the Devil. He gestures to the half-cube, which represents the half-truth of outer form. The figure seems to say, "This is all there is. The material world contains the whole truth."

The cure for this arrogant lie is hidden in the letter Ayin. The realization of the absurdity of the materialist's claim as sole possessor of the truth restores a balance to our perspective of existence. The lifted hand of the Devil bears the sign of limitation, symbolized by the planet Saturn. Yet the gesture itself is the holy sign of benediction of Orthodox Judaism. So, the message conveyed is that, through right use of the principle of limitation and discipline, bondage may be

THE HERMETIC QABALAH

conquered. The "joke" that causes the mirth is there for all to see.

In this Arcanum lies the secret of renewal. For if there was no limitation, there would be no manifestation, and it is in this realm of time and space that we must seek freedom from bondage.

The Devil in this key represents the archangel Auriel, the "Light of God." One must look beyond the veil of appearance to see beneath the illusion of the Tempter, and recognize the face of the Redeemer. Remember in Hebrew, Nachash (NChSh) the Tempter is 357 and this is the same number as Messiah (MShICh) the Redeemer. This sequence of numbers 3-5-7 holds special significance for Freemasons and refers to a pathway. Their sum, 15, is the number of this Tarot Key and of the holy name of God, Yah (IH), the first half of the Tetragrammaton attributed to the Supernal Sephiroth (Kether, Chokmah and Binah). This is the divine trinity represented by the emblem of the Eye in the Triangle.

After Jesus received his baptism from his cousin John, he went into the wilderness for a period of forty days. Forty is the number in Qabalistic symbolism that represents a complete cycle of consciousness. In this case it refers to a purging of consciousness by the three tests or temptations. These tests were said to be presented to him by the spirit. These three temptations represent the three great tests that every Adept must overcome:

  (1) Turn stones into bread – the Lie of Materialism;
  (2) Have all the people bow down before him – The Lie of Separation;

THE HERMETIC QABALAH

(3) Throw himself from the heights – The Lie of Mortality.

In the Book of Job, the Devil is represented as God's prosecuting attorney–the presenter of temptations. For without temptation and testing, there can be no triumph.

This path is assigned to the Renewing Intelligence. Here we seek to be reborn through the renewing of our mind. Our addiction to the desire to be admired, wealthy, or famous (symbolized by the three temptations) must be brought under control. These desires must be seen for what they are–manifestations of fear.

> *"Fear is failure,"* says an old ritual. *"Therefore, be thou without fear!"*

How do we overcome this fear? One of the attributions of this path holds the answer. Mirth. We all need to learn to laugh at ourselves. We need to learn to love unselfishly. Perfect love casteth out fear. Fear keeps us from trying. Only when we cease to try, to courageously attempt to improve and transform, do we fail. When things look like the Devil, then we need to love and to laugh—especially at ourselves.

Let us take a look at the Principle of Limitation. How can we use it productively, rather than reacting in a way that enslaves us? First, we utilize the principle of limitation when we select a goal. By doing so, we focus and activate all of our energy to achieve a purpose. This phenomenon is easy to observe in any successful endeavor. In truth, limitation is one of the critical factors contributing to success or failure.

THE HERMETIC QABALAH

When we study the Tree of Life, we begin by selecting one aspect before moving on to the next. In this manner, we utilize the Principle of Limitation to understand the entire Tree and the interrelationships of its many component parts.

Our subconscious minds, working beneath the surface of our awareness, makes the unobserved connections that later emerge, sometimes quite surprisingly as illuminations and new realizations.

These new realizations, in time, become the foundations for further revelations of inner and outer truths.

THE HERMETIC QABALAH

Chapter 29

*The 25ᵗʰ Path of the Letter Samekh
The Intelligence of Probation & Trial*

THE HERMETIC QABALAH

The 25th path is assigned to the letter Samekh and the Intelligence of Probation and Trial. Samekh is Hebrew for "tent pole" and is therefore viewed as the support of our house of consciousness. The test referred to is single-hearted devotion to the One and the purity of purpose that must be hers who would enter the Greater Mysteries.

In the initiation system of the True and Invisible Order, the 25th Path is perhaps one of the most dramatic and important. It forms the link between the Lesser and the Greater Mysteries and is associated with the stage known as the Portal.

After an initiate has taken the elemental grades and has roused into activity the various components of his physical/psychological make-up, it is necessary to ground and balance these parts. This is the "probation and trial" that is referred to in the Qabalistic attributions of this path.

A paradox exists here, for while these trials require zeal and persistence, the quality of receptivity to the true and higher Self is also most important.

In the Tarot Arcana, that of Key #14, Temperance, assigned to this path, expresses the essence of this work.

Hermes said, "Equilibrium is the secret of the Great Work." In Key #14 we see the Archangel Michael, symbolic of the Higher Self, pouring water on a lion, symbolic of the fiery zodiacal sign of Leo. With the other hand, he drops fire on an eagle, symbolic of the watery sign Scorpio. This balancing of opposites is

THE HERMETIC QABALAH

further emphasized by the name of this Key, Temperance.

According to the Random House Dictionary:

> "Tempering is to impart strength or toughness by heating...then cooling a substance (i.e. a metal) under controlled conditions."

For example, master sword-makers temper their blades using this process in the forging of a strong weapon. Psychologically, it refers to the process of balancing deficient or over-developed traits to a state of equilibrium. This is accomplished by both physical, objective conditions as well as by inner, subjective adjustments in the responses of our consciousness. This foundation is what is symbolized by the posture of Michael, who has one foot on the land and the other in the water.

This psycho-physiological tempering process is the key to the initiatory transformation symbolized by the path leading to the mountain of initiation and enlightenment. Note that it is guarded by the angel, who is symbolic of our higher consciousness.

This, our true Self, is an individualized ray of the Solar Logos. Thus, the One Ego is a living presence in the core of every human heart. It is this consciousness that performs the tempering, the essence of the Path of Probation and Trial.

The nature of the process is revealed by the stage of alchemy attributed to this path. It is "incineration," the purifactory action that sacrifices all immature patterns of error seated in our deep consciousness. These patterns are the result of misinterpretations of

THE HERMETIC QABALAH

experiences, our own as well as those inherited by us through the collective unconsciousness. Paul Case remarked that it takes about a year to purge these errors—if we are diligent, as mentioned in an earlier chapter.

The place to eliminate these erroneous patterns is after they have matured and been brought to the conscious level. Then we may deny them expression and replace them with seeds of truth. Little by little we will purify our consciousness until the point of critical mass is reached.

Part of this practice involves the inviting of the Higher Self to guide us on a daily basis. Ann Davies was known, at one stage of her training, to place copies of Tarot Key #14 all over her home and workspace. She even had one taped to her bathroom mirror so she would be reminded to invite the presence of her "Holy Guardian Angel" into her experience while she was brushing her teeth!

The Qabalistic Intelligence assigned to this path in the 32 Paths of Wisdom is called, as we have mentioned, the Path of Probation and Trial. Here is the idea of being tested. And, this is fitting, for it is this path that links the First and Second Orders or the Lesser and Greater Mysteries.

In an ancient esoteric text, we are told that the essence of this test is, "single-hearted devotion to the One." This devotion is based on the direct experience that vanquishes any skeptical doubt as to the objective reality of this great consciousness residing at the center of each of our consciousness. We are told later, in the same esoteric source, that it is this consciousness that

THE HERMETIC QABALAH

will determine whether we shall move from the "called" to those who are "chosen."

This same lesson is emblematically represented by the design seen on the reverse of the Great Seal of the United States, which may be found on any dollar bill. Here, we see the incomplete temple of consciousness represented by the unfinished pyramid. The cap-stone which completes and is the crowning glory of this edifice, is being lowered onto its pinnacle by the invisible hands of God. This divine consciousness is identical with our innermost Self, which has been laboring in the quarries of incarnations over many lives to perfect the personality to become a fit instrument for its manifestation. Here, is the secret reality behind the second coming of the Christ. When our personality has been prepared we become united with our Higher Self and may say, "My Father and I are One!"

Here, the last vestiges of separation are alchemically incinerated to reveal the true gold of the Self. This experience comes through Grace.

If we look at Tarot Key #5, The Hierophant we shall see a hint of this.

THE HERMETIC QABALAH

The two acolytes represent both our subconscious and conscious minds. The one who wears the red roses represents the subconscious. Note that this acolyte is actively reaching for the keys, symbolizing the attitude of active aspiration, engrained in our deep mind by our training in the Lesser Mysteries.

The Acolyte vested in lilies represents the conscious mind. His hands are clasped in prayerful adoration. He is the passive recipient of Grace. This is a reversal of the normal modes. Through this process we become receptive to the, "Knowledge and Conversation of our Holy Guardian Angel."

This is accomplished through the purification (symbolized in Key #14) of the water being poured upon

THE HERMETIC QABALAH

the lion and the consecration, symbolized by the fire poured on the eagle. This is the balancing of the vital soul of the aspirant.

The fire nature related to the zodiacal sign Leo, represented by the lion, must be purified. The Will must be transferred from the little ego, to the Christ within, the great lion of Judah.

The eagle is related to Scorpio and the sex drive. This faculty must be consecrated to the highest expression of aspiration. No longer can we afford the "dirtiness" and "immature" images and expressions of by-gone days. Thus, it is said, we must borrow strength from the eagle to soar to the sun.

THE HERMETIC QABALAH

Chapter 30
The 24th Path of the Letter Nun
The Imaginative Intelligence

Einstein once said, "Imagination is one hundred times more important than intelligence." Mystics (of which he, arguably, was one) would agree. For, it is imagination that allows us to see new possibilities. It was imagination that created humankind's walk on the moon–and beyond.

The initiate knows, however, that this faculty must be trained and disciplined. Then it becomes the universal

THE HERMETIC QABALAH

solvent. It is the imagination that alters the matrix of manifestation. It determines our paradigms and our reality.

Tarot Key #13 of the major Arcana, is Death. In general, death is viewed as a termination, a ceasing of existence. Yet, we die daily. We are not the same person, even physically, that we were yesterday. In fact, a baby's cells die at a rate ten times faster than an adult. Ageing is caused by not replacing cells!

The river in Tarot Key #13 flows toward the Sun. Many students of Tarot assume this key depicts the setting of the sun, but this is incorrect. The dawn is shown here. We are gazing at a new day, a new cycle—a new experience. Death makes this possible.

Initiates look at this process, not as a termination, but as a transformation. We must intellectually accept the idea of immortal life. This is the critical first step in opening ourselves up to the miraculous, transforming power of the Imaginative Intelligence. To facilitate this process we must analyze our fear of death. You can start by examining your attitudes. Do you avoid talking about or thinking about death? Why? Is it because unconsciously you fear it? Many initiates do. It has been said of initiates in ancient times that one of the gifts given by the Mysteries was the absolute freedom from the fear of death. How was this accomplished? Certainly not by avoiding all thought concerning the subject.

One might object and point out that it was easier for our ancient, less scientifically inclined brethren, to believe in immortality.
Many of our present day comrades rightly reject the "blind faith" allegiance that orthodoxy preaches with

THE HERMETIC QABALAH

outmoded doctrine. Though, to their everlasting credit, many materialists still work in accordance with the highest code of conduct, carrying on in the face of, to their way of thinking, total annihilation. This is an admirable trait worthy of heroes.

But initiates, while rejecting the position of blind faith, must still carefully study the process known as death. Modern day culture makes this very difficult. Consider the prevailing attitude against euthanasia. Freedom from pain and suffering is condemned. Death is looked on as either as a gateway to an eternal reward or damnation by the orthodox and total oblivion by the materialist.

This influence of the race consciousness must be counteracted by proactive, positive, specific actions. And this is an obligation for the initiate. As one who has entered the portal of initiation, we accept the task of dispelling these fear based conceptions of death. In this way, we become healers of humanity.

No one likes change. But, it is only through dying of the old (change) that we can be reborn unto a newer, more liberated life. While these newer, more enlightened concepts can provide much comfort during a personal episode of bereavement, we should not expect it will be easy to experience the death (transition) of a loved one. We experience loss. Even if we "know" that our friend or family member has departed on a journey of transformation, we also know that we will no longer be able to relate to this person in the same way we have become accustomed.

Change is the one constant of life and our imagination is the agent of that change.

THE HERMETIC QABALAH

Tarot Key #13 is attributed to the zodiacal sign of Scorpio. Scorpio is the Night-house of Mars and is ruled by this planet. It is the Mars energy, the reproductive force under the direction of our creative imagination (which is assigned to Venus) that is the source of the transformation that changes an aspirant to an Adept.

If we examine closely the skeleton in this Arcanum, we shall see two "twists" in the spinal column. This detail would be immediately obvious if skin and flesh were placed over the bones. We would see two contortions, one at the throat and one at the pelvis. These are the locations of the inner, sacred centers of the two planets involved in this process. The Venus center is located at the throat, while the pelvis is the site of the Mars center. In Egyptian paintings of the neters or gods, we see this same convention. Ancient Egyptian hieroglyphical art was strictly regulated by the priesthood. It is no accident that this detail is presented here.

This process is summarized by the ancient alchemists with the phrase; solve et coagula, dissolve and reform (a process we have seen to underlie many of the concepts outlined in this book). This practice is highlighted in an old mystery ritual where it is said, "These are the elements of my body, which I destroy so that I may create them anew!"

Key #13, Death; the Devil of Key #15; and the Holy Guardian Angel represented in Key#14 are identical. They simply represent three different methods whereby the Higher Self or Individuality prepares us for the experience of Union.
The 24th path on the ascent of the Tree of Life is the last path traversed before the Greater Mysteries and the grades of Adept are reached. Completion of this path

THE HERMETIC QABALAH

represents the overcoming the great Lie of Mortality and the experience of the Mystical Death.

Most people, spiritual aspirants included, identify the self with the personality. But this cannot be so, for the personality is constantly shifting and changing in response to the experiences of daily life. It is the very definition of impermanence. This shifting sand cannot be the foundation upon which we build the, "Temple not made with hands." Or is it? As the skeleton reaps the fruit of the field, so are the harvest of our personality experiences the basis for the eternal concepts that help purify our perceptions and perfect our vehicles for the descent of the Shekinah.

To do this we must change our paradigm. We must change our point of view in order to see clearly that the personality is but a tool—not the Self. Once again we must dissolve (break up) and reform. This comes, at first, as an intellectual assumption. But, if held consistently, it will transmute our very cells with the new pattern of immortality.

These patterns of aspiration and receptivity will activate channels in the etheric body through which we may receive the guidance of the Individuality. Through the practice of invoking the energy of our Higher Self, these alterations make it possible for the transformative high-tension energies (that normally would disintegrate these lower vehicles) to effect the mystical rebirth.

Thus, we must embrace the patterns of transformation, avoiding the tendency to hold on to that which no longer serves us and, in fact, may be holding us back. We must die that we may be reborn.

THE HERMETIC QABALAH

Chapter 31
The 23rd Path of the Letter Mem
The Stable Intelligence

The Stable intelligence is represented pictorially by the twelfth Arcanum of the Tarot, called The Hanged Man. It is concerned, at least in part, with the mysteries of time.

THE HERMETIC QABALAH

Time, as we normally refer to it is divided up into past, present, and future. But, in reality, this is just the way our self-consciousness deals with our manifested reality. Self-consciousness is designed to focus our one-pointed attention and cannot really deal with the concept of eternity. It is finite consciousness looking at infinity.

Subconsciousness, on the other hand, is not restricted to this view of time. It views time as cyclical and flowing. Who of us has not spent hours in a dream only to awake and find to our amazement that we have only been asleep for a few minutes?

The totality of time may only be viewed (on those rare occasions) when the flow of consciousness stops and we become aware of the eternal moment of now.

This last point is represented by the fact that the Hanged Man is suspended over a dry water-course. The stream of consciousness has been slowed down and then stopped. His head, which would have normally been submerged in the water, is free. He radiates the halo of Superconscious ecstasy and is completely emerged in the *Now*.

The 23rd path is the first path leading to the attunement of the consciousness of a Greater Adept. The symbolism of the Hanged Man shows how this state may be achieved.

First, the Hanged Man speaks to us of the Principle of Reversal. An Adept sees things differently that the man in the street. The average person has been seduced by the lie of outer causation. He is in a reactive mode, reacting to the forces, moment-to-moment, that he perceives to be outside of himself. These forces, he interprets, rule his life. His salvation is in how quickly

THE HERMETIC QABALAH

he reacts and how accurately he assesses the effect on his person.

Conversely, the Adept knows that the One Identity, expressing through self, is the Primal Will-to-good. This great consciousness is the author of all activities, conditions, and events. She also knows that through her own images, she establishes the matrix or foundation of all manifested events.

Dr. Paul Case often referred to the Hanged Man using the title of The Suspended Mind, pointing out that the figure resembles a pendulum at rest. Herein is the key to a great secret. Only when a pendulum is at rest, does it escape the swing, to and from, of reactive manifestation. When it has reached equilibrium, it can sense the very subtle forces present. Much of the time our minds resemble the activity of a drunken monkey. They rush madly from one image to another, at the mercy of habit, and out of control. One need only attempt to focus on one image for any significant period of time to observe how often and how fast the mind wanders. Most of us exert little control over this unruly servant.

Note that the dry water channel is a symbol of this control. It suggests to the subconscious mind that, not only can our thoughts be directed, but the flow of consciousness can be slowed down and calmed. This "suspension" results in the state known in the East as Samadhi. In this condition a perfect state of communication exists between the three modes of consciousness—they become one.

The Path of Mem connects the Sephirah of Hod, the intellect, to that of Geburah, the Cosmic Will. The grade of Greater Adept, assigned to Geburah is all about

THE HERMETIC QABALAH

aligning with the Will of the Divine. It is by surrendering our self-consciousness to the highest that this alignment seen in Key #12 is possible. The Hanged Man depicts a willing sacrifice made to the Divine.

We must consciously face and overcome the obstacles that are preventing this sacrifice. All of the Aspirant's training is brought to bear on the task of consistently and persistently detecting and eliminating these outworn patterns of consciousness and behavior.

We should be careful not to confuse the state of suspended mind with that of surrendered will or passivity. This confusion would render the Aspirant directionless at the mercy of the forces of imbalance. Instead we must affirm our alignment with the Cosmic Will at every occasion. This is part of the work of the alchemical stage of Incineration assigned to the letter Samekh about which we discussed in a previous chapter. In this stage of Putrefaction assigned to this path of Mem, the personal mind is seen for what it truly is—a temporary focusing of the Divine Will. Thus, the permanence of the separate personality is reduced to nothing. The true actor and identity is the Cosmic.

THE HERMETIC QABALAH

Chapter 32
The 22nd Path of the Letter Lamed
The Fruitful Intelligence

THE HERMETIC QABALAH

The next path we will discuss is the path of Lamed, represented in the Tarot by Key #11, Justice. This path leads from Tiphareth, the Sephirah of the Individuality and the powers of Imagination, to that of Geburah, the sphere of the Cosmic Will. It deals with the grades of Lesser and Greater Adept.

When one looks at the Tarot Key, the first thing that normally attracts the attention is the balance scales. The Scales of Justice is a phrase with which we are all familiar. Its symbolism goes back to the time of ancient Egypt --- if not before. In the initiation ritual known as *The Book of the Coming Forth by Day*, commonly called the *Book of the Dead*, we find it. Here, in the Judgment Hall of Osiris, it symbolizes rectitude. In this part of the ritual, the life of the candidate, symbolized by his heart, is weighed against the Feather of Ma'at, the goddess of Truth. From this, we get the ideas of the Last Judgment, etc.

The great Egyptian adept, Hermes Trismegistus, tells us that: "Equilibrium (i.e. dynamic balance) is the secret of the Great Work." This equilibrium reflects our inner sense of what is right and what is wrong. Not in a legal material sense, but that inner knowing of what is fair and right.

Additionally, this equilibrium refers to other more esoteric, microcosmic states. Alchemy has, for one of its goals, the manifestation of the mysterious Elixir of Life. This substance is supposed to grant physical immortality, according to some or at least, greatly prolong life and assure perfect health according to others. It is like the Holy Grail depicted in the popular movie *Indiana Jones and the Last Crusade*. While the movie is a work of fantasy, the fact remains that aging is a product of the breaking down or (catabolism)

THE HERMETIC QABALAH

processes of the body gaining ascendency over anabolism, the building processes.

Hence, aging and age related illnesses are not so much about dying as it is about our lowering rate of replenishment—of not being reborn.

Paul Case wrote that, as we get older, our desire to hold on to conditions is a major contributor in the ageing process. In fact, he explained that the subconscious response is a result of the accumulation of dead cells which have outlived their usefulness, causing arthritis and related ailments.

The secret to prolonged life and health is connected to balance and harmony, i.e. equilibrium. And this state is controlled by our habitual mental imagery. We control our blood chemistry by our thoughts and emotions. Fear or anger, for example, has been conclusively shown to influence our health. Even our choice of food is mostly a mental selection. Psychosis is primarily the product of brain chemistry.

For the Hermetic student Justice is intrinsically linked to the concept of Karma. Karma, as I have written elsewhere, is a tendency toward equilibrium. It is instructive rather than punitive. Any action on any level sets in motion a reactive equalizing energy. We choose how we respond to this energy. We may react in an unconscious manner, and often times, overcompensate. This tends to lead to further imbalance. Or, we may move beyond reaction and effect, to the proactive and causative plane and reinstate equilibrium. We evolve our mastership by becoming more and more adept and precise in this process—more and more exacting in our observance of Cosmic Law. In this way do we intelligently align our personal patterns

THE HERMETIC QABALAH

of thinking and acting, with their macrocosmic counterparts. As above---so below. We seek to become a mirror of the cosmic equilibrium. This is accomplished by putting into conscious practice the Law of Inner Causation. We actively embody the fifth statement of the Pattern on the Trestleboard, which states:

> I recognize the manifestation of undeviating Justice in all the circumstances of my life.

This recognition is not a realization of punishment, or guilt or fear, but recognition of consistent justice and control and security. We create our freedom and triumph. Through the volitional power of Geburah and the Mars force, we energize those patterns that we have formed through the imaginative faculty of Tiphareth and our Higher Self.

The zodiacal sign of Libra is attributed to this path. Librans are noted for the finesse in which they approach any situation. Their qualities of subtleness and indirect application are most effective when forming suggestions to the deep consciousness. The direct, commanding approach of say an Aries, many times results in resistance. The subconsciousness then obediently manifests this expectation, making the situation more difficult. This path necessitates a diplomatic approach. Yet, in our culture, the direct, head-on approach is honored as forth-right, open, and honest. Wheras, the subtle, diplomatic approach is considered slightly devious, manipulative, and dishonest. The Warrior is held in higher esteem than the diplomat. This is a symptom of the Lie of Separation, and its strength in our collective unconsciousness. In reality, a more balanced approach is what is usually called for. This is symbolized again by the energies depicted by the sword and scales in the 11th key of Tarot.

THE HERMETIC QABALAH

The alchemical stage associated with this path is that of Sublimation. This term translates as "change across" and refers to the process of channeling an urge, drive, or substance into a higher avenue of expression. This is the opposite of suppression. When we suppress or "push down" on a form of energy or behavior and refuse to give it expression, the energy or urge to express does not go away. In fact, often times, it increases just as pressure increases in a boiler if it is allowed to boil with increasing heat but not channeled into some form of action. This results in an explosion. True, we may turn off the fire and the energy will dissipate, but then we will have lost a valuable resource of power. On the other hand, we can use it to turn the blades of a turbine and provide the needed electricity to light a city. The same may be said of consciousness.

We may, for the sake of example, have a natural sexual urge. For some reason we choose to not allow it an acceptable expression and, instead try to suppress it. Here is a recipe for disaster, for we cannot deny expression to one of Life's greatest drives. If we attempt it, it will find expression in spite of our efforts, perhaps in an unacceptable form. But, if we are trained in the disciplines of the Mysteries, we may direct this great energy into the higher channels of artistic and mystical creativity. We may sublimate it.

For this reason, all forms of spiritual development prescribe a certain period for abstinence. Note, we stated this was for a certain period only and that the energy must be directed into another, higher expression for this period. After the goal is obtained, this scaffolding may be discarded. This is one of the meanings behind St. Paul's statement "...when I became a man, I put away childish things..."

THE HERMETIC QABALAH

Sublimation is the result of equilibrium. It is the outcome of the balancing of opposites until the balance pans of the scales are at rest.

In relation to the attribution of the sign Libra to this path, it is interesting to note that, in earlier versions of the Tarot, Keys #8, Strength and Key#11 were switched as a blind. Thus, you had Strength, a picture featuring a large, red lion being attributed to Libra and Justice, depicting a figure holding a balance scale assigned to Leo. The obvious switch was, was well—obvious.

However, there is a deeper reason for this transposition. In the inner alchemical process of the initiatory experience, there is an interplay or relationship between the heart center assigned to Leo and the kidneys and adrenals, assigned to Libra.

In the Anahata Chakra or subtle heart center, the blood is charged with the Solar current. When properly controlled it causes the adrenals to alter the chemistry of the blood through the cleansing activities of the kidneys. This obtains a state of equilibrium that energizes certain nerve currents related to the experience of awakening discussed earlier in the chapter on the 27th Path.

This awakening has to do with the Saturn force or Kundalini. Saturn is exalted or finds its highest expression in Libra (It has been my experience that astrological exaltations most always have to do with the alchemical process). The planet Saturn has to do with the power that finds its expression in limitation and discipline. The training that relates to this aspect of the work requires generous portions of both.

THE HERMETIC QABALAH

The activity of the Kidneys in relation to this process is one of the reasons all valid systems of spiritual development emphasize the need to drink sufficient quantities of liquids, especially water.

The matter of discipline should extend to the formulation of new constructive habit patterns. These new habits must replace the old, unproductive ones. One of the most common mistakes made by people seeking to break a habit is the failure to replace it with a new, constructive one. The energy that was bound up in the old pattern is suddenly freed and unless it is channeled into a new pattern, it will usually revert back to the old habit, causing a relapse. Occasionally, it will energize a latent, destructive pattern. Therefore, care should be taken to consciously channel the energy into a new, more productive lifestyle.

THE HERMETIC QABALAH

Chapter 33
The 21st Path of the Letter Kaph
The Intelligence of Conciliation

In Hebrew, the name of the letter Kaph means grasp or comprehension, in contrast to Yod, the letter which precedes it, depicting the open hand in the act of giving.

THE HERMETIC QABALAH

Various titles have been assigned to this path: The Rewarding Intelligence for Those that Seek; the Intelligence of the Desirous Quest. But, the one most used in the Hermetic Qabalistic system is that of the **Intelligence of Conciliation.**

My teacher once explained the relation of these three titles by pointing out their location on the Tree of Life. On one end we have the Sephirah Chesed, the seat of expression of Compassionate Love and the Masters of Righteousness, the Tzadikim. This state of consciousness is the ultimate goal of every Adept. For here the greater initiate becomes one with the essential nature of the Cosmic—Love. This is the reward of those who seek.

The path arises from Netzach, the seat of the Desire Power. As I have previously stated, it is desire that powers the engine of aspiration. It is assigned to the element of Fire, and, like fire, desire is a good servant but a dangerous master. It must be controlled and channeled, not undisciplined or repressed.

The secret of channeling this power to arrive at the goal of identification with Cosmic Love is found in the third title—Conciliating. Conciliation, balancing equilibrium, is the secret of the Great Work.

Some Schools of Psychology popular in the 1950's advocated the freeing of the subconsciousness to promote mental health and fulfillment. While this idea sounds great, these schools advocated a recipe for catastrophe. The subconscious mind is a totally amoral creature. It isn't good or bad. It doesn't understand these concepts. The subconscious is represented in the Bible as the Garden of Eden. Symbolically, good and

THE HERMETIC QABALAH

evil were introduced by the Serpent of Wisdom and the fruit of the Tree of Knowledge.

The subconsciousness is a good servant, but a terribly fatal master. The principle of balance must be firmly imprinted on it. The Qabalah transmits this message in many ways. Some examples are the Star of David with its balancing interposition of opposite triangles. Another is the pillars of the Tree of Life.

In this last example we should note that it is the Middle Pillar of Consciousness that is said to be the path to higher realization. Here, are seen the five Sephiroth (including Da'ath) that correspond to the levels of consciousness, from the Divine in Kether to the elemental in Malkuth. At each level, it is the One Consciousness that focuses and balances the different expressions of creation.

The Desire force in Netzach is one of the most powerful expressions of transformation. It can be selfish, destructive and damaging, or when properly directed, can remake our world into the image of Divine Love. It is our self-consciousness that controls these formulations. Through this power we will develop the power of empathy (feeling with others). This power helps us move beyond our personal limits of self-consciousness to the freedom of Superconsciousness. In this state, we experience and express the pleasure of being a vehicle for the fulfillment of the cosmic desire.

This path is represented by The Wheel of Fortune of the Major Arcana of the Tarot. Fulfillment comes by harmonizing with the ebb and flow of cosmic cycles and tides. Every successful gambler intuitively realizes this, feeling when it is time to walk away from the table. What, to them is personified as Lady Luck is, in reality our unconscious perception of the cycles of manifestation. The gambler's ability to do this, results in their experience of *Wealth and Poverty*, the "contraries" assigned to this path in the *Sepher Yetzirah*.

Our concepts of universal supply in our subconscious patterns determine the effectiveness of our powers of manifestation. On the Pattern on the Trestleboard, the sentence assigned to Chesed (and the planet Jupiter), is:

> "From the exhaustless riches of its limitless substance, I draw all things needful, both spiritual and material."

This is a statement of truth. Is this light shining into the garden of our subconsciousness, or is the garden of our deep mind riddled with the seeds of guilt and fear-born patterns? Probably there is a little of both. We are not separate from the rest of humankind and the patterns of lack has been a self-fulfilling prophesy based on a lie for a long, long time. Further, the idea that wealth and abundance is somehow unspiritual complicates matters. While we should guard against conspicuous consumption, it is necessary to have an adequate supply of resources to achieve our purposes. It is a question of priorities. When do we have enough? Is it enough to fulfill or manifest our desires? And what do we desire? An important question, is it not? Life is an adventure in awakening and fulfillment if it is pursued correctly. Let us not be like Ebenezer Scrooge before the spirits visited him, investing his whole being in things that rust and decay. Let us, rather, act in accordance with his realization, "The business of man is mankind." He who recognizes the reality of the inexhaustible supply will realize this truth.

THE HERMETIC QABALAH

How then may we find this path to fulfillment? By looking for and discovering the truth of things. Ignorance is not bliss. It is the mother of fear and fear is failure. It is by seeing beneath the surface of appearance that the liberating truth is revealed. It is not the intellectual patterns of limitation and lack that enslaves us. It is our strong emotional reaction to these perceptions. When we act from the center of all that is, we break the chains of bondage and throw off the shackles of ignorance. As scripture puts it, "**If God is for us, who can be against us?**"

This path leads the initiate to the grade of Exempt Adept and the Sephirah Chesed. One of the attributions of Chesed is memory. How does this faculty of consciousness relate to the higher awareness of an advanced adept?

As we probe within, we encounter the accumulated lies and errors transmitted down the ages via our collective unconsciousness. There, as I have discussed previously, are the true original sins, which must be redeemed before we can truly realize our destiny of God-consciousness.

The desire nature is energized and focused by intense aspiration and shines upon those patterns of error, revealing them for what they are—lies, mistakes, and misconceptions. Then, by following the stream of consciousness backwards to our origins, we "remember" the truth about our divine nature and the truth of spirituality, immortality, and unity. We remember the truth that we are all expressions of the divine light, the truth that we are manifestations of Light in Extension, and individualized rays of the One Light of Love.

THE HERMETIC QABALAH

Chapter 34
The 20th Path of the Letter Yod
The Intelligence of Will

The 20th path links Tiphareth, the Sephirah of the Individuality (the Higher Self) and the Imagination to Chesed, the Sephirah of Love, Compassion, and Cosmic Memory.

Its microcosmic correspondence is to the Virgo region of the body, the upper lobe of the small intestines. This area is connected to the critical aspect of the alchemical process known as "the discovery of the First Matter."

In the grade of Lesser Adept, assigned to Tiphareth, the spiritual experience is Knowledge and Conversation of the Holy Guardian Angel. This refers to union and expression of the Higher Self with and through the personality.

In the path of Yod, this awareness and activity is stabilized and grounded so that it becomes the dominant state of consciousness. The First Matter, macrocosmically, is that primal substance known as Mezla. This descends, like a lightning flash from the Primal Will, rooted in Kether and is channeled down, in turn, through the other Sephiroth. This is symbolized by the letter Yod which is the foundation of every letter in the Hebrew Flame alphabet. This energy is sometimes referred to as Chai, the Life-force. Its

THE HERMETIC QABALAH

connection to the Virgo region of the human body is one of the most important keys to spiritual alchemy. Poetically, this is expressed in the description of the birth of the Christ, where we are told that the, "Christ is born of a Virgin in Bethlehem, the House of Bread."

Virgo is unique among the signs of the zodiac, in that it is the only sign where its ruler is also exalted. This planet is Mercury and, in the Western Mysteries, Mercury is symbolic of the Intellect and the power of attention. In this phase of the Hermetic science, attention is utilized to increase the effectiveness of the assimilation process. These processes are associated with the Virgo region of the body. This attention maximizes the amount of radiant Chaiah energy extracted from the food we eat. This energy then charges the Chyle found in lymph, eventually making it available to awaken the alchemical centers or chakras. The result of this awakening transforms the ordinary consciousness from Homo Sapiens to Homo Adeptus by the confection of the internal Philosopher's Stone of the Wise. This "stone" is a physical structure contained within the body of the Adept. Paul Case once wrote, (and I paraphrase) "It was one of Nature's ironies that the greatest achievement of Man depended upon the simple act of charging one's food before eating."

By assimilating increased "Philosopher's Mercury," (not to be confused with the liquid metal, which is very poisonous), into the personality vehicles our subconsciousness, we alters them so that we may interrupt and register the higher tension currents of the astral light. When this is accomplished, the Adept comes into contact with the continuous broadcasts of Wisdom being transmitted by the Inner School.

THE HERMETIC QABALAH

This is depicted symbolically by Tarot Key #9, The Hermit, assigned to this path:

Here we see a white-bearded elder (the typical portrayal of the Ancient of Days) shining the light of wisdom to guide all sincere seekers on the Path. This harkens back to the mythological story of the ancient Greek sage who would search through the night, holding his lantern high, looking for an honest man. This story highlights a critical quality of character so necessary for a seeker of wisdom. That is honesty. The ability to be in integrity with others but also to be completely honest with oneself is essential. This prevents the aspirant from wandering down the seductive path of self-deception

THE HERMETIC QABALAH

that derails so many seeking the illumination of the Self.

It is a well-known saying in the Hermetic/Alchemical work, that:

> "The Great Work is the operation of the Sun and the Moon with the aid of Mercury."

This is perhaps easier to understand as follows: the transformation of the human being into an Adept is the interaction of the three modes of consciousness. The Superconsciousness is the mode that does the work (Sun). The Subconsciousness is the mode that is the subject of the work (Moon). Mercury, is the Self-conscious mode, is the agency through which it is accomplished.

How does this happen? It is not only by accumulation of the right knowledge but a critical orientation as to the use of this knowledge. As we have often stated, there is only one key whereby one may safely enter the temple of the Mysteries and that is service to God, Humanity, and our own Higher Self. The desire to know in order that we might serve is the root of all activities of spiritual transformation. The accumulation of knowledge without this orientation leads to the inflation of the ego, which is the great test of the Lesser Adept. This inflation leads to projection of short-comings and faults on the teachings, teachers, and fellow aspirants.

This ability to be honest with oneself requires a keen development of the power of discrimination, which is the ability to see fine shades of difference and the outcomes likely to result from each when chosen. The sword represents this quality. In Tarot, this is represented by the sixth arcanum, The Lovers, and its letter Zain, the

THE HERMETIC QABALAH

Sword. The sign Gemini connected to this key is also ruled by Mercury, as is Virgo.

In alchemy this path is assigned to the stage called Dissolution. This term refers to the ability of consciousness to reduce all forms back to their original root so that they may then recombine for more advanced efficient expressions.

Physiologically this refers to the complete digestion of nutrients to a liquid state so that they may be "taken up" by the lymph system using the process of assimilation. This extract of the subtle essences is what provides the energy to transform the body into that of an Adept.

Remember, discrimination is an exercise in being selective. To be selective we must be aware of what is being offered and, at least, be receptive to the idea that in food and air there resides subtle essences. Thus, we make the decision to draw from these substances more to charge our bloodstream. Subconsciousness acts on these suggestions and activates the operation of the Sun. The Chyle, a milky white substance found in the lymph and made up of emulsified white blood cells and oil soluble vitamins, then becomes energized. This comprises the "earthy" (Virgo) portion of a tripartite substance. The chyle flows into the Super Vena Cava from whence it passes through the heart. Here, it is charged with Solar Prana, channeled through the Sun Chakra. This substance, at this point, referred to as the Green Lion, now flows into the Pulmonary Artery and into the lungs. Breathing formulas then charge this substance with the vital, subtle, atmospheric prana by a process known as the "fixing of the volatile." This fixing only occurs if the earthy/solar base is already present in the blood, as it is needed to anchor the action of the

THE HERMETIC QABALAH

prana. Breathing exercises alone will not accomplish this process.

When the operation is complete, the substance becomes the Red Lion or alternatively, Potable Gold.

This entire process falls under the direction of the self-conscious mind, which uses the powers of imaging and symbols to direct the subconsciousness to perform the various transformations. In the East, Patanjali outlined this process in his *Yoga Aphorisms*. In the West, this is part of the Hermetic Qabalah known as the Unwritten Qabalah or Alchemy.

Digest and assimilate. As initiates, we may direct our subconsciousness to extract many times the normal amount of this *first matter*, for use in altering our vehicles. All of this action occurs in the Virgo region of the body.

The fulfillment of this work will be discussed further in the chapter on the next letter—that of the path of Teth.

THE HERMETIC QABALAH

Chapter 35
The 19th Path of the Letter Teth
The Intelligence of the Secret of
Of All Spiritual Activities

The doctrine of the Trinity has vexed generations for centuries. Theologians, convinced that their one interpretation is the only correct one, have argued their point, enforcing it with fear and even death. How does the initiate interpret this doctrine?

First, we do not believe there is more than one God. Even our pagan brothers and sisters agree in that. There is only one cosmic power manifesting in many, many ways. The Trinity is explained as three main modes of function or expression—not identity. For example, each of us, likewise, has multiple roles. I, for one, am a father, an author, a brother, etc. That is the way I relate and the roles I fulfill. There is only one of me, a unique specialization of the Cosmic. God may manifest as the creator, or as the recognition of fulfillment in human form, or as the ever-changing presence in each human heart. Still, it is forever ONE and the ALL.

Initiates experience, in three modalities of illumination, the grades of Adeptship. In Lesser Adept we realize God as the essential reality of ourselves. In Greater Adept

THE HERMETIC QABALAH

we realize the Cosmic Will as the total motivating power manifesting through us. And, in the grade of Exempt Adept, we remember and embody the essence of Divine Love. These become our reality or rather we realize that this has always been reality. It becomes the essence of our every thought, feeling, and motivation.

The triad of Adeptship, of Individuality, is comprised of the expression of the three Sephiroth of Tiphareth, Geburah, and Chesed. These are linked by three paths. We have discussed two of these paths, Lamed and Yod, in the preceding two chapters. With the 19th Path of the letter Teth, we complete this triangle.

THE HERMETIC QABALAH

Tarot Key #8, Strength, attributed to this path, represents the Law of Suggestion. It is this law, indeed, that is the Secret of all Spiritual Activities. This law states that our manifestation of consciousness is amenable to the directions originated from higher level of consciousness, provided these suggestions are formed correctly. This applies to sub-molecular intelligences through all manifestations to that of the Divine.

It is through the Law of Suggestion that the mighty power of the subconsciousness is directed to make the extremely subtle alterations that transform an Initiate into an Adept. This secret is revealed in the symbolism illustrated in Tarot Key #8, Strength.

The 19th path is one of the three reciprocal paths on the Qabalistic Tree of Life. That is, they are horizontal and are said to balance the two Sephiroth they connect by allowing the energy to move both ways. According to the tradition, these three paths hold the key to enlightenment. Looking at the three Tarot Arcana assigned to these paths, we can see that it tells us a secret. The uppermost is the 14th path, assigned to Daleth and Key #3. This is assigned to creative imagination and the desire force. The middle path, (i.e. the 19th, which we are presently discussing) is assigned to the letter Teth and is symbolic of the Law of Suggestion. The third or lowest path is the 27th assigned to the letter Peh, which depicts the stage of spiritual unfoldment known as Awakening. This stage is illustrated by the 16th Key of Tarot, The Tower. Meditation on these three keys reveals to us that when the desire force is directed consciously utilizing the Law of Suggestion, we attain enlightenment.

Examining Key #8, we see that the Lady, symbolizing our creative imagination, has harnessed the great power

THE HERMETIC QABALAH

of Nature (symbolized by the Red Lion) using the garland of roses. The Red Rose is a symbol of desire and love. Yet to channel and direct the energy of the cosmic force, this desire must first be altered and adapted by human consciousness. Notice that the roses have been woven into a chain. Through this artifice the lady holds the lion's mouth open and articulates or gives it expression.

Some systems of so-called spiritual development mistakenly advocate bypassing the self-conscious mind. What must be done, in reality, is to increase the efficiency of this mode of consciousness so that it effectively gives suggestions to the subconsciousness which will accurately reflect the directives of the True Self.

These directives enable the subconsciousness to manufacture in the body the Red Lion, as discussed in the previous chapter. This potable gold energizes the interior metals. This activation, in turn enables the Serpent-fire (Kundalini) to rise up the spinal channel, rousing into activity these centers. This sacred energy, as the *Emerald Tablet* explains, first ascends and then descends, transforming the quality of consciousness of the aspirant.

Kundalini has been described as the serpent power and there are three letters in the Hebrew alphabet that reflect this symbolism—Teth, Nun and Samekh. The student is encouraged to lay out the three Tarot Arcana attributed to these letters (Key 8, 13, & 14) and meditate on them.

Teth is a pictograph of a serpent coiled at rest. In most people this represents the "normal" state of the

THE HERMETIC QABALAH

Kundalini. It is the Serpent-fire potential waiting to be awakened at the proper time by the Law of Suggestion.

Nun (especially apparent in its "final" form), while the name means "fish," represents a serpent crawling or rising. It is associated with the idea of fruition and reproductive abundance.

Samekh, the letter represented by the 14th Key of Tarot, Temperance, represents a serpent biting its own tail. This diagram was known by the medieval alchemists as the Ouroborus. This symbol was taken to represent the completion of the Great Work and the state of enlightenment.

The Law of Suggestion, represented by the path under discussion is the foundation of this process. Thus, the name given it in the *Sepher Yetzirah* is The Secret of All Spiritual Activities.

The Red Lion represents the vital life-energy given expression by our liberated and purified subconsciousness. This liberation is affected through discipline and directed desire.

In the next chapter, we will begin our exploration of the paths linking the Second Order to the Third.

THE HERMETIC QABALAH

Chapter 36
The 18th Path of the Letter Cheth
The Intelligence of the House of Influence

This is the first path that unites the Greater Mysteries with the Supreme Mysteries. The Supreme Mysteries, also known as the Third or Invisible Order is represented by the three Supernal Sephiroth.

These three have always been considered part of a different archetypal reality than the seven Sephiroth below. For this reason, they are said to be separated by the Great Abyss.

Attainment of these grades is only possible by sacrificing all personal desires that are incompatible with the one desire—to be a vehicle of service to the Divine. The aspirant must be imbued with the consciousness of Oneness in all she says, thinks, feels or does.

But note that even after this condition has been realized, when incarnated in a body and functioning through a personality, the Masters still are subject to the illusion of separation. They, however, are not deluded by it and see it for what it is—a necessary focusing of consciousness as a unique expression.

THE HERMETIC QABALAH

In every act of creation the principle of limitation is involved. As consciousness proceeds from the inception of an idea through the process of manifestation, a progressive series of choices are made. Without this limiting selection, creation on any level is impossible.

The vehicle of human consciousness is the tool for this process in regards to the evolution of the aspirant. This path is, therefore, is referred to as the Intelligence of the House of Influence.

As the first path across the Abyss, it is traditional that the advancing initiate take on him or herself the Oath of the Abyss, whereby every thought, feeling or action is viewed as a vehicle of service to God and humanity. The Famous Rosicrucian vow now evolves from, "I will look upon every circumstance of my life as a direct dealing of God on my soul, to "Every circumstance of my soul is a direct expression or vehicle of the Divine." This is not really a change, but an internal recognition of the Truth.

In light of this oath, the attribution of the stage of the Great Work to this path of Separation is puzzling. However, this becomes clearer when we view the Individuality of each human being as a separate, unique expression of the All. Each of us is a ray of the One Light, which experiences and evolves in a totally different expression. The point to remember is that consciousness does not originate within us, but expresses though us.

The path of Cheth connects Geburah, the sphere of the cosmic Will to Binah, the Sephirah of the Neshamah, the Divine Mind. The Neshamah is the universal soul– the Great Mother. In Binah she is referred to also as

THE HERMETIC QABALAH

the Dark Mother because at this level she is still Unmanifest potential. She is the spring from which manifestation flows forth. This is Isis who no man can unveil. She will, however, unveil herself to the one who has aligned himself to the Divine Will. Then she becomes the revealer of the deepest mysteries of existence.

The letter-name Cheth may be translated as a fence or enclosure. As such, it refers to the separation or defining of an arena of expression for any given creative act. The principle of limitation or restriction related to the planet Saturn is assigned to Binah. This is further explained if we examine the symbolism of Tarot Key #7, The Chariot, which is attributed to this path.

THE HERMETIC QABALAH

Here we see the Self, expressing as a specialized aspect of consciousness, driving the chariot of personality. This idea of the personality as a vehicle for evolution is a theme that exists in most of the sacred literature of the world. In the Qabalah, it is epitomized as Ezekiel's Chariot and is referred to as the "Work of the Merkabah or the Chariot." This meditative exercise utilizes the personality as a vehicle through which the ecstatic Qabalist receives visions of the higher consciousness. The personality is the Chariot—not the Self. Through the influence of this path, we seek to establish a fully conscious linkage with the Cosmic Soul.

As we become aware of this flow from the highest, our role as the Mediating Intelligence (assigned to Tiphareth) becomes clearer and more potent. This is the origin of the idea that one newly crossing the Abyss will discover a new Word that embodies his illumined realization. Crowley, for example, designated Thelema (i.e. Will) as his word of the Aeon. This does not occur only once in every age. Instead, it happens to every initiate that achieves this level of awakening.

THE HERMETIC QABALAH

Chapter 37
The 17th Path of the Letter Zain
The Intelligence of the Disposing Intelligence

The 17th Path carries the influence from the Divine Mind or Neshamah across the Abyss to Tiphareth, the sphere of the Higher Mind or Individuality. It is designated by the Hebrew letter Zain (the Sword) and is titled the Path of the Disposing Intelligence in the *32 Paths of Wisdom*. The corresponding stage in the alchemical Great Work is that of Fixation.

A sword, in the language of symbolism in the Western Mystery Tradition, relates to the ideas of discrimination and judgment. Like the Principle of Separation in the preceding chapter, it deals with making choices.

As mentioned repeatedly, there is but One Will that of the Divine—the Cosmic. While we do not possess free will, we do have freedom of choice. We can choose from among many options. Some are aligned to the One Will—and we prosper. Some are opposed to that same One Will—and we learn. The ability to distinguish between the often times, fine shades of differences and options requires discrimination. This is the ability to see both sides of any issue or decision. The quality of being able to see this two-sidedness is a quality

THE HERMETIC QABALAH

associated with the zodiacal sign Gemini, attributed to this path.

Zain, the sword cuts away the veils of the deluding perception of the Divine Will. We have only to look at the poverty, disease, violence and hate rampant in our society to see the product of indiscriminant choices made by ourselves in ages past.

The remedy for this chaos is alignment to truth. "And the Truth shall set us free."

How can we implement this solution? The answer lies in the utilization of the Law of Suggestion and The Law of Response. Used together we may "see" the connection between the three modes of consciousness.

You will recall that the Law of Response states that every level of consciousness is governed by a superior one. Further, that every state of creation is a direct result of the states that preceded it, tracing back eventually to the original cause that set the universe into motion.

The Law of Suggestion explains how our subconsciousness relates to our self-conscious mind. The subconscious level of mind is completely and at all times amenable to suggestions originating at the level of our self-consciousness. However, a certain problem plagues the dynamic between the subconsciousness and self-consciousness. That is, that subconscious reasoning is limited to the syllogistic logic of the deductive mode.

Wrong premises coming from the limited perspective of the self-consciousness will lead to wrongly directed manifestations. One of the goals of the training in the esoteric schools is to remedy this defect by bringing the

THE HERMETIC QABALAH

self-consciousness under the overshadowing guidance of the Individuality, the true and infallible Self. Basically, the subconsciousness is freed from suggestions originating at the self-conscious level unless those suggestions are approved by the Individuality. In Key #6, we see the depiction of this ideal relationship.

As related to the Tree of Life, the Man represents the powers of Hod, the Woman, Netzach, and the angel, Tiphareth. Note that the light of blessing from the True Self creates a harmonious, effective, and fulfilling relationship. Thus, the name of the arcanum is The Lovers.

THE HERMETIC QABALAH

This path and the letter Zain deal with *Discrimination*.

Ann Davies, during a Thursday Night Class, once told her students that many sorrows connected with love relationships are rooted in false expectations. Perhaps this is the reason why nearly fifty-percent of all marriages end in divorce within the first five years. After the relationship matures the chances of success are much better.

As the aspirant advances through the stages of initiation represented by the Tree of Life, this careful discrimination, the measuring, weighing and consideration of the various traits of the personality vehicle becomes more critical. This inward reflection and elimination of detrimental characteristics and the reinforcement of beneficial ones refine the personality into an instrument that may safely mediate the higher powers.

No longer will the painful process of trial and error be the predominant method of growth, but the immediate reflexive discrimination will take its place.

The enlightened insight that is the product of this process reveals insight into the truth that is clear, detailed and provides a sure compass for further awakening. The establishment of a balanced and loving relationship between the three modes of consciousness, as depicted in Tarot Key #6, will provide a working paradigm for the adjustments necessary to progress in the Great Work.

THE HERMETIC QABALAH

Chapter 38
The 16th Path of the Letter Vav
The Intelligence of the Triumphant & Eternal Intelligence

The path of Vav connects the Sephirah Tiphareth and the sphere of the Individuality to the Sephirah Chokmah, that of the Divine Father and the Cosmic Life Power,

THE HERMETIC QABALAH

Tiphareth relates to the Christos or the Divine Son. It is the consciousness of at-one-ment. This is reinforced by the meanings connected with the letter name Vav. Vav means nail and a nail connects or unites things. In Sanskrit this idea is conveyed by the word Yoga. Yoga is the group of disciplines that unite the Divine Consciousness with that of the personal.

In the Tarot, this is represented symbolically by the fifth arcanum, The Hierophant. The title Hierophant means literally, "He who explains the sacred symbols," or "Expounder of the Mysteries." In the Eleusinian Mysteries this Hierophant was the chief officer. It was a hereditary office, passed down from one generation to another, usually from father to son, but sometimes to a daughter. The hierophant never left the inner precincts of the Temple. This was the Adytum where the inner mysteries of initiation were communicated. This officer was simply an outer expression of the inner teacher within each one of us. This teacher is described in the Bible as the still, small voice of God.

The qualities needed to approach and gain access to this inner teacher, (who in reality is the true Self) are depicted in the postures of the two acolytes pictured in the Tarot Key.

As mentioned in a previous chapter, the one vested in roses, represents our emotional nature. He is striving, earnestly and actively aspiring, as shown by the figure reaching for the keys. The one clothed in lilies, representing the intellect, is in an attitude of adoration. This represents a suspension of the negative, critical mind in favor of inner revelation. We must be open-minded to the Hierophant or our access will be cut-off.

THE HERMETIC QABALAH

Thus, it is said in Christian theology, that the only unforgivable sin is to deny the Holy Spirit.

Aspiration and Adoration, represented by these two acolytes, are essential tools for the initiate. They aid in our inner receptivity to the most abstract intuitions. The posture of these two figures indicates an assiduous development in both the art of receiving and of giving. This awareness of the flow of teaching, primes the pump of enlightenment. We would desire to know that we may serve more effectively. This silent service to our fellow brothers and sisters is not to be underestimated. The change initiated by a few trained, enlightened consciousnesses acting as vehicles for Truth is indeed potent! It is the cause of evolution for it is an alignment with the Cosmic Will. It is the expansion of the true compassion that flows through the path of Cheth that we have just studied. This is the destiny of the true initiate—to become a Light Bearer, as depicted in Tarot Key #9, the Hermit. He who receives from above that he may transmit to all below.

The source of all instruction is the One Teacher within, represented by the Hierophant. Every circumstance, event, or relationship is grist for his mill. He grinds slowly and exceedingly fine. When the initiate looks back on her life, she will find that nothing has been wasted. No experience is accidental or superfluous. All has been done to develop those qualities of character that are needed to complete the Temple not made with hands, the instrument of the Hierarchy of Light.

These ideas have to do with the qualities of the letter Vav, the nail. They point out how all life experiences are related, connected and united. It is this interrelationship that the still, small voice reveals to us when we turn inside to hear that revelation. Hence in

THE HERMETIC QABALAH

the *Sepher Yetzirah*, Vav is assigned to the power of hearing. Hearing, even on the inner levels concerns the property of sound. Sound is the transmission of patterns through a media. These forms are the foundations of manifestation. As Patanjali says:

"Through sound the world stands."
This idea relates to the doctrine of the Word of Creation—the so-called Logos. In Genesis it is emphasized by the phrase, "And God said..." Even today's physicists refer to this moment as the Big Bang. There was no atmosphere, but there was still a basic, vibratory motion or activity. This is the initial impulse—The Lost Word, the Spell of Making.

This theory of vibration presents interesting implications. Since any given vibrating frequency, if strong enough, should be accessible anywhere in the Cosmos, it becomes a real presence in each person's life. All that is needed is a proper receiving mechanism. Adepts have realized this mechanism for millennia—consciousness. Through this medium they can open themselves up to the advanced teaching being broadcast from the higher levels of the hierarchy. Further, during acts of Theurgy, these practitioners may become instruments for the reception and expression of those powerful centers of consciousness known as the archetypes. This channeling of the archetypal energies forms a critical part of what is known as the Greater Mysteries. This is symbolized by both The Hierophant and The Hermit in the Tarot.

Yet, we must penetrate beyond the symbolism of the Hierophant to that of the Emperor–the next path.

THE HERMETIC QABALAH

Chapter 39
The 15th Path of the Letter Heh
The Constituting Intelligence

The path of Heh carries the influence of the Cosmic Life Power into the area of focus that we call the Individuality. The Constituting (or "setting in order") activity manifests as the ability to observe phenomena (be it physical or mental) and to identify patterns. This leads to a perception of order and, more importantly Divine Intent.

THE HERMETIC QABALAH

In the Tarot, this aspect is represented by The Emperor. Even a casual examination of this figure will reveal that his posture appears awkward and artificial. The position of his body together with the cube he sits on, reveal an interesting composition—a triangle above a cross. This is the alchemist's conventional symbol for Sulphur, one of the three great Alchemical Principles.

Diagram # 23   The Alchemical Symbol for Sulphur

Sulphur is that mode of the one substance that initiates, activates, or promotes action. As depicted in Key #4 of the Tarot, it shows the activity of the Superconscious mind when functioning at the self-conscious level of expression. Note the position of the head. It is only seen in profile. Add to that his white beard and hair, and we have a picture of what is described as the Ancient of Days. This is the traditional magical image of the Sephirah Kether, used in the Practical Qabalah– except for one detail. In the Zohar, he is described as being all right-faced. Thus, he should be looking to the right. But in Tarot Key #4 he is "all left-faced," i.e.

THE HERMETIC QABALAH

looking toward the left. What is the significance of this detail?

We are told that in the image of the Ancient of Days, as a pictorial representation of Kether, that the left side represents the Unmanifest. This part of God is the unknowable source of manifestation. The right side therefore represents the known works of God, the luminous garment of effects.

Applying this symbolism to The Emperor, the ruler or "He who sets in order," we find we are shown the cause of manifestation. Further, one will note that the Emperor is looking toward the North. This direction is, traditionally, the place of greatest symbolical darkness. This is because in the northern hemisphere the Sun never ventures north of the ecliptic. The North therefore symbolizes the future and its mystery.

Meditation on these symbolic ideas reveals that manifestation is the result of the Divine within each of us, marking out order from the infinite possibilities of the future.

We must penetrate beyond the visible face of effects to the invisible, hidden countenance of cause, to understand the Path of Heh. We must penetrate the pure, luminous darkness that is the womb of creation. For in this darkness we shall find that the source of all light is the dwelling place of Truth–the object of our quest and the pattern of our actions. As Ann Davies once taught, "In that darkness all separation, all individuality, all distinction ceases."

The Emperor symbolizes the faculty of reason. Reason is the power to discern patterns, relationships, connections, and causation. This is done through

THE HERMETIC QABALAH

observation of phenomena, both internal and external. Hence it is rooted in the activity of human self-consciousness since the primary role of this mode of consciousness is to observe and form premises or theories about what is observed. And, since all causation is really internal, it is this mode that holds the key to creation—to mastery. When this activity serves the Higher Self, true magic occurs!

Know Thy Self, (which really means to become one with Thy True Self) was the primary directive given to initiates in ancient times. This has not changed and is still the imperative for today. As *The Book of Tokens*, tells us:

> "What Thou seekest, truly that thou art!
> The treasure thou journeyest afar to find,
> Is the Jewel of Eternity in thy heart of hearts."

Modern psychotherapy and ancient meditative disciplines both agree that the aggressive, proactive process of looking at the One Self, and one's motives and behavioral responses, is critical to inner health. Conflicts both drain creative vitality and also provide material for productive examination. This is symbolized by the alchemical stage of Calcination, which is attributed to this path. Calcination requires the practice of self-honesty, a virtue that is rare. Initiates cannot afford the luxury of self-deception.

This is a difficult challenge, but our True Self will give us no task we are unable to complete. If there is no challenge, there is no triumph.

The symbol of the armor, helmet, and gauntlets relate to the attitudes of strength, action, and initiative. But

THE HERMETIC QABALAH

note they are worn by a figure which symbolizes the eternal Cosmic Will within each of us. To help us understand this we may meditate on the following passage from Mabel Collins' book, *Light on the Path*:

> ...Stand aside in the coming battle, and though thou fightest be not thou the warrior. Look for the warrior and let him fight in thee. Take his orders and obey them. Obey him not as though he were a general, but as though he were thyself, and his spoken words were the utterance of thy secret desires; for he is thyself, yet infinitely wiser and stronger than thyself. Look for him, else in the fever and hurry of the fight thou mayest pass him; and he will not know thee unless thou knowest him. If thy cry meets his listening ear, then he will fight in thee and fill the dull void within. And if this is so, then canst thou go through the fight cool and unwearied, standing aside and letting him battle for thee. Then it will be impossible for thee to strike one blow amiss. But if thou look not for him, if thou pass him by, then there is no safeguard for thee. Thy brain will reel, thy heart will grow uncertain, and in the dust of the battlefield thy sight and senses will fail, and thou wilt not know thy friends from thy enemies.
>
> "He is thyself, yet thou art but finite and liable to error. He is eternal and is sure. He is eternal truth. When once he has entered thee and become thy warrior, he will never utterly desert thee and in the day of the great peace he will become one with thee... [Light on the Path, by Mabel Collins, p.9]

THE HERMETIC QABALAH

The Emperor is enthroned on a cube of stone, symbol of Eternal Truth. When our observations are rooted in Universal Truth, we become one with the true ruler of all there is. Aries, attributed to this path is called the Day House of Mars. This refers to the action of the fire of God awakening to full activity in the interior stars (chakras) located in the forebrain area of the head. These centers comprise the third eye or the adytum. When these are completed they bestow on the individual the ability to alter the vibration of the environment and to rule it.

THE HERMETIC QABALAH

Chapter 40
The 14th Path of the Letter Daleth
The Luminous Intelligence

The path of Daleth is the highest of the three reciprocal paths. It mediates and balances the supernal energies of the Sephiroth Binah (the root of the power of Water) and Chokmah (the root of the power of Fire). Therefore it relates to the age-old theurgical practices of purification and consecration.

Purification means literally to make pure and uses the symbol of water to represent the mind-stuff. That is why in the ceremonies of the Western Esoteric Orders, we use the phrase purify *by* water. We purify or cleanse the channels of our consciousness through the images we hold in our mind-stuff. We control that instrument via the Laws of Suggestion, Response, and Inner Causation.

To consecrate, means "with sacredness or holiness." This refers to the act of aligning with the Holy Spirit, symbolized by fire. This power is not subject to our personal control. We may only become vehicles for its Will. In recognition of this fact, we declare in ceremonial that we "consecrate *with* fire."

THE HERMETIC QABALAH

The power that unites these two modes of expression is symbolized by Da'ath, or Gnosis. This path links the Sephiroth representing the Divine Mother to that of the Cosmic Father. This symbolism manifests through many modes of interaction; the opposites of magnetic and electric, form and force, etc. Throughout all levels of interaction, we see this interplay in creation. The point of balance is Da'ath. In path-workings or guided meditations, the temple of Da'ath is traditionally depicted as an empty chamber with two doors, one in the West and the other in the East. This temple represents the portal wherein the Yekhidah or Indivisible One enters into the drama of cosmic manifestation on the one hand, and the experience of ecstatic union with the All on the other.

THE HERMETIC QABALAH

Remember the meaning of Daleth, the letter assigned to this path is "doorway." This portal is related closely to the symbolism of the womb. The womb is the gateway from which issues the beginning of manifestation. Note that we use the word manifestation and not life. For Life exists before the womb and persists after the womb. It is this flow of this essence that is our true identity and by which we can say with Jesus, "Before Abraham, I was," and, as it is said in *The Book of Tokens*, "And when worlds are but a memory, I shall be!"

All of the symbols in Tarot Key #3 relate to this creative process. The very name Daleth, spelled *DLTh* reveals this. *D* is the gate whereby the energy of life enters into manifestation. *L* relates to the balance that must be present to sustain creation. And, finally *Th* represents the defining, limiting power of Saturn that concretizes the energy of consciousness into manifestation.

The Empress represents this process. She is pregnant, enthroned in a plush, fertile garden, next to a pool of water. These are all symbols of the gates of life.

But Daleth has also been called the Tomb or the gate of the next life. This energy that sustains life is the same power that supports us on the Unmanifest side of the process also.

To this path the Qabalistic contraries of Wisdom and Folly are assigned. Although "contraries" are normally considered as opposites, they are, in reality, complimentary partners in the process. As *The Kybalion* states:

THE HERMETIC QABALAH

> ...Everything is Dual; everything has poles; everything has its pair of opposites; like and unlike are the same; opposites are identical in nature, but different in degree; extremes meet; all truths are but half-truths; all paradoxes may be reconciled." [p.32]

The Empress wears a necklace of seven pearls. Besides referring to the awakening of the Chakras, this necklace is symbolic of an important Qabalistic concept. Pearls are sacred to the goddess Venus. Seven, on the Tree of Life is the number of the Sephirah Netzach, which has as one of its attributions, Venus. These two symbolic attributions highlight the importance of the desire power (also assigned to Netzach) and it role in the creative process.

Further, this Tarot Key is said to hold the secret of the creative process through the use of the creative imagination. This secret relates to the fact that images held in our consciousness form the matrix or basis that is manifested in our environment.

Remember, the Law of Inner Causation states:

> "We create our reality on a moment-to-moment basis through the images we habitually hold and choose to energize with our desire force."

Mere intellectualization is not enough and is, in fact, sterile. We must desire in order to create! The intellect provides the form, but the emotions provide the power.

Where does this craving, this yearning come from? It is not personal in nature. It does not originate within us, but flows through us. It is Cosmic in origin. Our imagination is a perfect vehicle for the universal

THE HERMETIC QABALAH

creative process—if we let it be. This occurs when we align our desire with the Cosmic Will, which is symbolized in Astrology and the Qabalah by Mars. This is one of the meanings of the ancient myths concerning the marriage of Aries and Aphrodite and that of Isis and Osiris. It is the dynamic produced by the interaction of our conscious and subconscious minds. Its origin, however, is the Superconsciousness.

In the *32 Paths of Wisdom*, the path of Daleth is referred to as the Path of the Luminous Intelligence. This brings to mind the saying of the Mystery Schools, "I am Isis, and no man has lifted my veil." The meaning behind this statement is that the true Hierophant or revealer of the Mysteries is Nature and the Inner Consciousness itself.

These Mysteries are the revealed wisdom that is known directly by those who have developed the capacity to contact the Divine within. This is the true purpose of any valid initiatory system. The initiate is trained and actively working to remove the necessity for any intermediaries—anything that may once have been necessary for his awakening, but now has been outgrown. If these become crutches, they must be cast aside—but only at the proper time. Then, as St. Paul said, "We see, face to face."

The Master Initiate working at this level provides the forms that are born out of the womb of creative consciousness for the benefit of all humankind. They become a mediator for the Cosmic.

Paul Case in his early writings pointed out that copper, the metal associated with this path and sacred to Venus, is the word Nechash in Hebrew. This word has a value in Gematria of 358. These digits, you will note,

THE HERMETIC QABALAH

are part of the famous *fibernaci series* or the golden mean ratio. When pronounced as Nachash, it means "serpent" and refers to the serpent of temptation in the Garden of Eden. This refers to the serpent-power, whose raising is critical to the illumination experience and the making of the Philosopher's Stone. 358 is also the value of *Messiach* or Messiah, the anointed one.

It is also interesting to consider that the Venus Center, known as the Vishudhi Chakra in the East, is also known as the Gate. When the Serpent-power is spontaneously aroused, in many cases it does not ascend further than the Venus center. Those who have experienced this phenomena report feeling the sensation of a "hole in their throat." [See "Kundalini: Psychosis or Transcendence" by Dr. Lee Sanella]. For the initiate who is trained in the correct methods, the "gate" is opened and the energy ascends into the brain where it awakens the higher centers and gives access to the inner hierophant.

These individuals are then able to communicate with the *Frater Rosae et Aureae Crucis,* a Brother of the Rose and Golden Cross.

THE HERMETIC QABALAH

Chapter 41
The 13th Path of the Letter Gimel
The Uniting Intelligence

There is a tradition in the Qabalah that states the 13th path is the last path of ascension up the Tree of Life. Clearly however there are two other paths, that of Aleph and Beth (the 11th and the 12th). The answer to this apparent contradiction is that these last two path only flow downwards. Thus, the 13th Path of the Uniting Intelligence is the only way across the Abyss that links to the Primal Will in Kether. To unite with this Will and act as its agent for the rest of creation is the ultimate goal of all mysticism.

This path unites the Ego or Individuality (True Self) of the aspirant to the God-head. Through it we may identify with the Yekhidah or Indivisible Self.

The ability to "walk" the Path of Gimel, in actuality, is dependent on fully experiencing the qualities of Chokmah and Binah, Cosmic Force and Cosmic Form.

Tarot Key #2, The High Priestess, represents this fact symbolically.

THE HERMETIC QABALAH

Get a good representation of this arcanum from either the B.O.T.A. or Rider-Waite deck and examine it in detail. Here is one of the clearest examples that the symbolism of the Tarot Major Arcana is based on the Qabalah. In this case, the symbolism of the Tree of Life determines the composition of the design.

The figure wears on her head a crown, symbolic of Kether (which is Hebrew for "crown.") Her blue garment flows down, symbolic of the 13th path itself. Her inner garment of white emphasizes the fact that the essence of this path is identical with the uniting power of Kether. Below her feet is the yellow colored pavement, symbolic of Tiphareth. To top this off, on her breast is an equal-armed cross, one of the symbols of

THE HERMETIC QABALAH

Da'ath; the mysterious invisible Sephirah located just where the 13th path crosses the 14th.

W.G. Gray, in his book, *The Ladder of Lights*, suggests that Da'ath is, in fact, the expression of the redeemed and exalted Malkuth.

Da'ath's spiritual experience is described as the vision of the Empty Room, and refers to the mystical truth that, at this level, no outward symbols are adequate to describe the illuminating realization of union. This experience is what the great 18th century mystic Louis Claude de St. Martin termed "reintegration." It is the full merging of identification with the Cosmic without losing the personal identity of self-consciousness.

Aleister Crowley described it as discovering your True Will. By this I think he meant the discovery that our personal will is a unique expression of the One Will of the Cosmic. We become, therefore, the "keeper" of the Universal Truth. As such, we "receive" this Wisdom, which is one reason Qabalah is referred to as the "received tradition."

This is a function of the feminine polarity which is symbolized in Tarot by the High Priestess, attributed to this path. This function is further reinforced by the numerical value of the letter Gimel, which is three. Three is the number of the Sephirah Binah, the root of Water and seat of the Great Mother.

Water has always been symbolic of the nature of mind and the mind–substance. The reflective nature of this element connects it with the power of memory. It is also interesting to note that when remembered in a dream, a symbol often will be reversed, inverted or "flipped."

THE HERMETIC QABALAH

This is exactly the way images are seen when reflected in a pool of water.

Water is an apt symbol for other reasons. It flows in currents and reflects only when clear, pure and calm. It can dissolve obstacles and flush barriers. Most importantly, it takes on the shape of any container and when its vibration is slowed (i.e. cooled), it becomes solid.

When the initiate reflects the supernal mode of consciousness into the mirror of the subconsciousness a spiritual transformation takes place. When we "remember" we are part of this stream of awareness, we become one with the creative power of the Cosmic (before it enters into the restriction of differentiation). Thus, the title of this path given in *The 32 Paths of Wisdom* is the Uniting Intelligence. Participation in this level of awareness requires a complete awakening and balancing of the interior sensorium, which is the true goal of spiritual alchemy. The few individuals who have achieved this, known in our tradition as Masters of the Wisdom, exercise control over the manifestation process. Their works appear miraculous to the rest of us. The senior of these is known as the Ipsissimus or "One who knows himself (or herself) best.

The Ipsissimus becomes one with the Source of all things, beyond time and space and all limitations. Many have thought this experience to be a complete merging with the All, resulting in loss of identity–a sort of consciousness of an emptiness or void. But we are taught otherwise. The Masters affirm that far from being filled with a void, they feel filled with the awareness of all things and love.

THE HERMETIC QABALAH

Void is Bohir in Hebrew and by Gematria equals the number 13. Remember, this is also the number of Unity (Echud) and Love (Ahevah).

THE HERMETIC QABALAH

Chapter 42
The 12th Path of the Letter Beth
The Transparent Intelligence

There are two paths on the Tree of Life that traditionally carry energy only one direction. Both the 11th and the 12th carry energy *from* Kether but not *to* it.

When considering the 12th path, it is very helpful to meditate on the second statement of The Pattern on the Trestleboard:

> "Through me, its unfailing Wisdom takes form in thought and word."

This statement taken together with the path's title of The Transparent Intelligence reveals many interesting points. Transparent is defined as that which lets the light pass through unimpeded. A perfected personality lets the light of Truth and of the Superconsciousness pass through with as little distortion as possible. This is our goal.

Most individuals, even though they are of good intent, tend to be translucent, meaning, they unintentionally "color" or "distort" the wisdom of the higher.

THE HERMETIC QABALAH

Individuals that are opaque are as rare as those who are transparent. These individuals have cut off their connection with their Higher Self.

When one strives to become transparent he discovers that, when we desire to express that higher consciousness and we focus our consciousness through acts of active attention we find our true destiny–that of service to the One Self as a vehicle of Healing, Wisdom and Love. But, with this realization comes no sense of egotistical self-importance. Rather, one realizes what Jesus meant when he said, "I do nothing of myself. It is the Father within me who does all things."

THE HERMETIC QABALAH

Look at Tarot Key #1. Observe that the Magician's uplifted arm is receiving power from above. It is a symbol of the focused will. The wand is colored white to show that it has been purified. This energy he is consciously transmitting to the subconsciousness, symbolized by the garden below.

Key #1 and the letter Beth are attributed to the planet Mercury. Mercury is unique in astrology in that is the only planet to both rule and also be exalted in the same sign–Virgo. It has been my theory, for some time that "exaltations" invariably relate to the process of spiritual alchemy. The Virgo region, as we have explained elsewhere, is assigned to the upper lobes of the small intestines. It is here that acts of concentration (symbolized by Mercury) supercharge the earthy part of our food and as the nutrients are passed into the lymph system by the lacteals, the Chyle is altered. This milky, white substance carried in the lymph is called Virgin's Milk by the alchemists. This is the first critical step in the physiological alteration process that leads to the manufacture of potable gold.

The letter Beth is one of the Hebrew double letters and, as such, has one of the pairs of Qabalistic contraries or opposites assigned to it, that of Life and Death.

I am often asked by students how they may purify their consciousness so that it becomes transparent. The secret lies with these opposites and the Qabalistic principle, "Attention Gives Life." When an unwanted reaction occurs in our habitual responses, how do we deal with it? It is immature, so we certainly don't want to reinforce it. Psychologists will remind us that behavior that is repeated is being reinforced. Since emotion is the power of manifestation, we should not reject our undesired patterns with unbalanced

THE HERMETIC QABALAH

vehemence, for this waters the weed with our emotions. Rather, we must first examine the underlying need. Is it based on fear, insecurity, or greed? Is this underlying need based on fact or illusion? If illusion, what is the truth? If it is true, let us logically be proactive rather than reactive in our response. Then we deal with the undesirable pattern by gently switching the focus to a pattern that will balance and replace the "weed." To continue our analogy, let us water the flowers and let the weeds dry up and blow away.

Is this repression? No, it is quite the opposite. Repression would be watering the weed and then vigorously forcing it down, away from the surface, burying it so that its seed can germinate. This never works. Indeed it reinforces the error and it will manifest more potently in an uncontrolled and unexpected manner.

Be proactive! Water and expose to the sunlight the patterns you wish to see manifested. Make it a conscious decision to calmly, with confidence remove your energy from the patterns of falsehood and replace them with those of Truth.

Plant reinforcing seeds by reading the Holy Writings of all religions, "The Book of Tokens," "Light on the Path," and similar inspirational works. Don't accept these writings uncritically, for that is fundamentalism and leads to fanaticism and imbalance. Instead use them as the basis of critical consideration and contemplation.

You will find as you enter into this practice, you will become an instrument through which some aspect of

THE HERMETIC QABALAH

Truth will shine. Or, as the Pattern on the Trestleboard expresses it, "Through me its unfailing Wisdom takes form in thought and word."

THE HERMETIC QABALAH

Chapter 43
The 11ᵗʰ Path of the Letter Aleph
The Path of the Fiery Intelligence

Aleph, the first letter of the Hebrew Alphabet has no pronunciation. It is simply (unless pointed) the sound of a sigh–"ahhh." As such, it is a proper symbol of the Life-breath. This is the expression of that which begins all creation, the out-breath of God.

As a word, it means "Ox," an ancient symbol of agriculture and herding. These activities were the first step in creating civilization, because until early humans could count on a dependable source of food in a single area, they could not build cities or villages. They could not specialize in one vocation, but were forced, as hunters and gatherers to follow the herds and forage for food.

This letter then represents the beginning of the Quest. Even its number is "1", the first number in the sequence.

THE HERMETIC QABALAH

As in the path of Beth, discussed in the previous chapter, the path of Aleph only brings energy from Kether, not to it.

The word Fool comes from the Latin follis, a bag filled with air–or a "wind-bag," the figure of the Court Jester. It was customary in medieval times for this individual to satirize and act as the in-house comedian and critic. Although this role could sometimes involve risk, the Jester was supposedly immune from reprisal. He was considered to be "touched in the head," meaning he was touched and protected by the gods. Later, the figure was transformed into that of the Divine Innocent, personified by Parsifal in the quest for the Holy Grail (another container of spirit). Thus, we have the container of wind seeking the container of spirit and the holy essence. Note that the word air or wind is used

THE HERMETIC QABALAH

both in the Bible and the Qabalah as a symbol for life and spirit. Here is a profound connection that deserves meditation.

We are each "containers of spirit" and, as such, are Grail Seekers. Ann Davies once pointed out that the Hebrew word for atmospheric air is Aveer. This word is linked by Gematria to the proper name Uri, son of Hur (or Ben Hur). This reference is found in the Old Testament Book of Second Chronicles. Hur is the Hebrew variant of the Egyptian god Horus (Khoor), the son of Isis and Osiris. Horus is attributed, in his aspect as a Sun god to the sixth Sephirah, Tiphareth. This is the true Self within each of us. It is the Divine Innocent that searches for the Grail and is identified as the Christos within each seeker. This is further reinforced by the name of the grade of a new initiate, Neophyte or a new plant in the garden of wisdom.

When an initiate has opened himself to the paths of Aleph and Beth, he may become part of the supernal, creative process by serving as an agent of cosmic form flowing to Binah and Force flowing through the path of Aleph to Chokmah.

In the text of the *The 32 Paths of Wisdom*, the 11th path is referred to as Saykel Matzokhtzokh, the Fiery or Scintillating Intelligence which mirrors and reflects the dazzling Divine Light of Kether. This path links the Primal Will of Kether to the Life-force of Chokmah. Thus, in the "Big Bang," of creation Kether represents the singularity, while Chokmah is the primal explosion itself. Kether represents the potential of the creative process–the seed. Chokmah is the active expression of that potential.

THE HERMETIC QABALAH

Paul Case pointed out many times that "0" is symbolic of the Life-breath before any restrictions of force or form. It has neither beginning nor any end. It precedes all processes and remains when all is completed. It is the Alpha and the Omega. The figure of the seeker or Quester can be either the Neophyte or the Ipsissimus, the first step and the completion.

The Fool's affect is that of a joyful adventurer, drawing his energy from the spiritual sun. He directs it through the Cosmic Will, symbolized by his staff, guided by the imagination represented by the Eagle on the flap of the wallet of universal memory. The goal is seen by the Quester as he looks toward the heights. To this ideal, this fulfillment, he is offering the white rose—a symbol of desire purified—desire fulfilled.

THE HERMETIC QABALAH

Chapter 44
The Mystery of Theurgy

The hero in one of Dion Fortune's stories from the book, The Secrets of Dr. Taverner has this to say:

"She was more than royal, she was an Initiate!"

What is this calling, the achievement that Dr. Taverner speaks so highly?

In the final analysis, it is a person that has undertaken the demanding, self-sacrificing process of reshaping, balancing, awakening and perfecting the consciousness, to the end that it may serve as an instrument for his or her higher and True Self.

"I desire to know, that I might serve."

This is the goal of true initiation. Further, as mentioned repeatedly, it is the only safe motive for pursuing the path of initiation. All other motives lead to self-deception and delusion. For the personality is built up during the course of an incarnation in reaction to life's experiences. These experiences teach us many lessons and develop many skills, but in the final analysis are not constructed on the firm foundation or

THE HERMETIC QABALAH

balanced plan that is necessary for the higher tension energies of initiation.

One who seeks to become an effective servant of Life must tear down, reshape, and build "anew," according to a pattern of balance. The secret of this work is revealed in the Psalm 127, where it is written:

> "Except the Lord build the house,
> they labor in vain who build it."

It is the direction of the Inner and True Self that is required in this work. The personality then becomes a servant for the healing of humanity. In this way we may view it as the highest, most noble calling to which one may dedicate oneself.

In this book we have attempted to show how the system of the Tree of Life of the Hermetic Qabalah can be an instrument for a complete system of initiation. This is usually the foundation of the ritual systems provided in a lodge of the Western Mysteries or a system of deep and powerful meditational exercises. In this way a sincere aspirant may tread the path of spiritual unfoldment.

The method used in this combination is known as Theurgy. This word translates, roughly, as Divine Working. It has been, in certain circles, unjustly derided as a dubious, dangerous, and forced path of development. This is largely undeserved. True, it is faster than that of simple meditation or devotion. But it is powerful and, if followed correctly, more effective in perfecting the personality vehicles for service to God, Nature, and Humanity.

THE HERMETIC QABALAH

The basis of Theurgy is the linking of one of the universal archetypes to the personality of the initiate through a series of symbols and images. This symbolic bridge acts as an energy transformer to "step-down" the power of the archetype so that it may be safely received by the aspirant's consciousness. The selection of the particular archetype and its associated energy is always done according to a balancing system so that all parts of the individual's consciousness receive stimulation and balance.

In this book, each path and its proposed goal have been discussed. It is hoped by the author, that a firm foundation for spiritual progress has been set forth. However, the value of a group of like-minded, spiritual aspirants must not be undervalued. We encourage sincere dedicated aspirants to seek initiation with a reputable lodge of the mysteries when they feel they are ready. For advice in this selection, they may contact the author at lvx.org, or a similar organization such as Builders of the Adytum or Servants of the Light.

I now leave you with this traditional blessing:

> "May you dwell beneath the shadow of His wings, whose name is Peace. Sub Umbra Alarum Tuarum, Jehovah.
>
> Paul A. Clark, Steward of the Fraternity of the Hidden Light.

THE HERMETIC QABALAH

Chapter 45

The Pilgrim on the Path

I hope that we have demonstrated in these pages that the system of the Hermetic Qabalah and its master diagram of the Tree of Life is not only an instrument to explain cosmology but is a valuable tool in understanding the journey known as initiation. Initiation is not an event as many may suppose. It is a process which, when undertaken sincerely, leads from natural humanity to that next step in the evolutionary process known as illuminated humanity.

By aid of the Tree, the sincere aspirant throws off the delusions of the Great Lies of Materialism, Separation, and Mortality and emerges triumphant as a witness of the truth and light of Spirituality, Unity, and Eternity. She does this not only for herself, but that she may serve in the healing and awakening of all humanity.

This Pilgrim of the Path treads alone but is never alone. For as he travels he is guided by all of his companions of the hidden ways, those who have gone this way before

THE HERMETIC QABALAH

and have turned to shout encouragement and shine their light on the path to guide him. An inner communion exists, a secret, invisible Order that spans the globe, encompassing all those who seek to know the mysteries of life that they might master them in order to serve their brothers, sisters, and all of humanity.

The fact that their motive is in accord with the Primal Will of the Universe makes them incredibly powerful. Wisdom must be developed. For with this power comes great responsibility.

THE HERMETIC QABALAH

Appendix

Diagrams of the Tree of Life

THE HERMETIC QABALAH

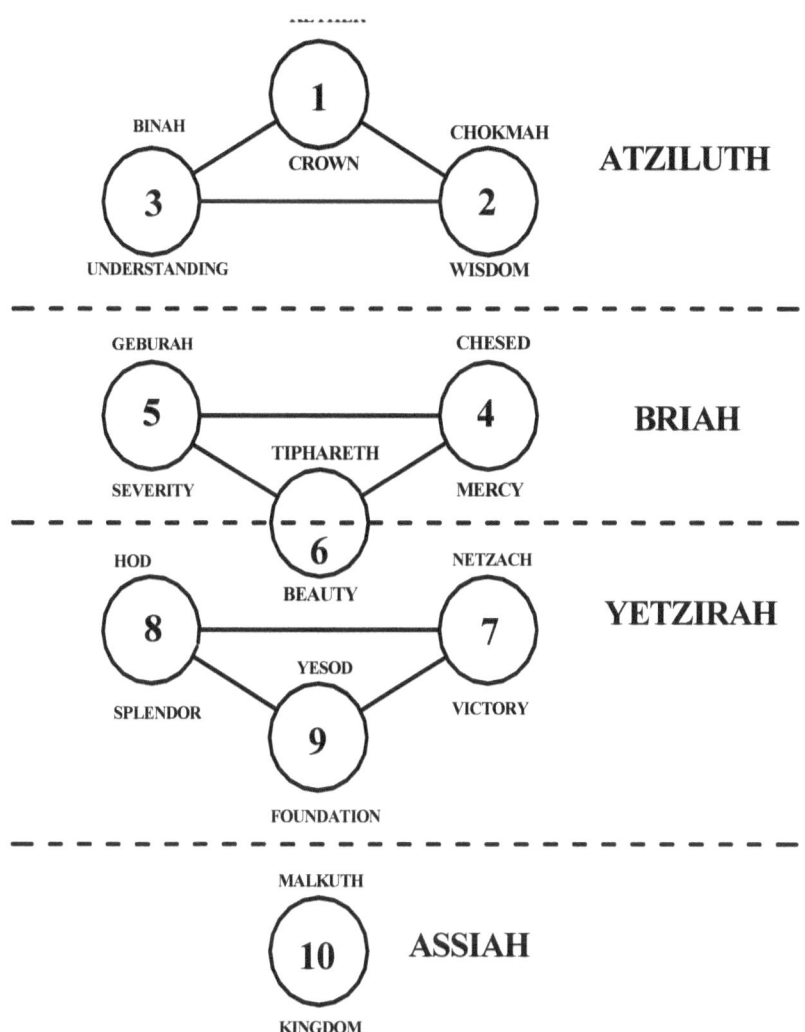

Diagram #24   The Tree in the Four Worlds

THE HERMETIC QABALAH

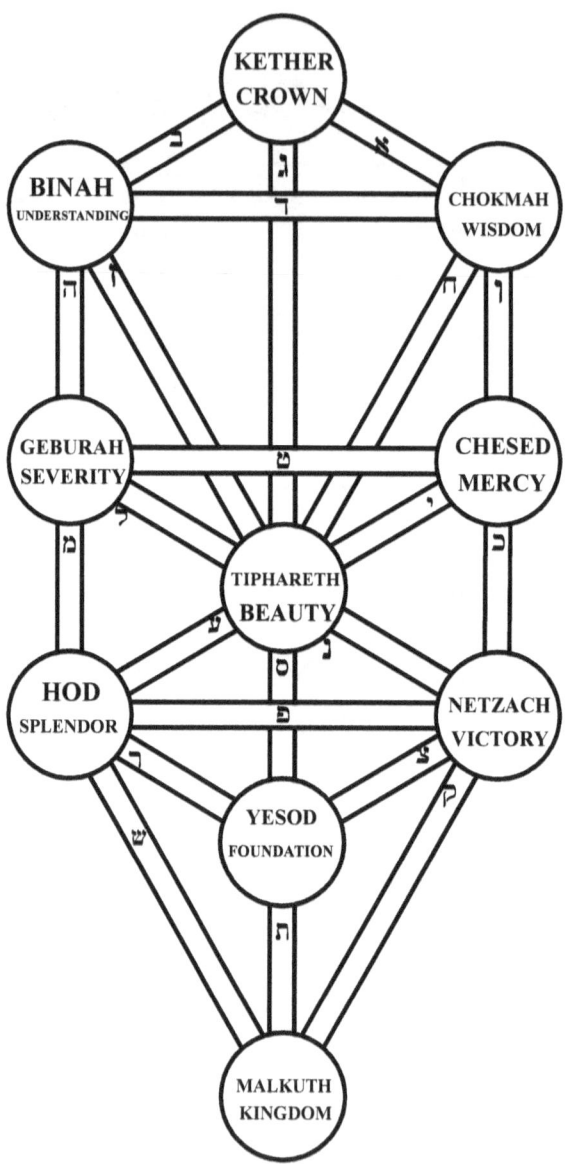

Diagram #25   The Tree of Life and the Paths

THE HERMETIC QABALAH

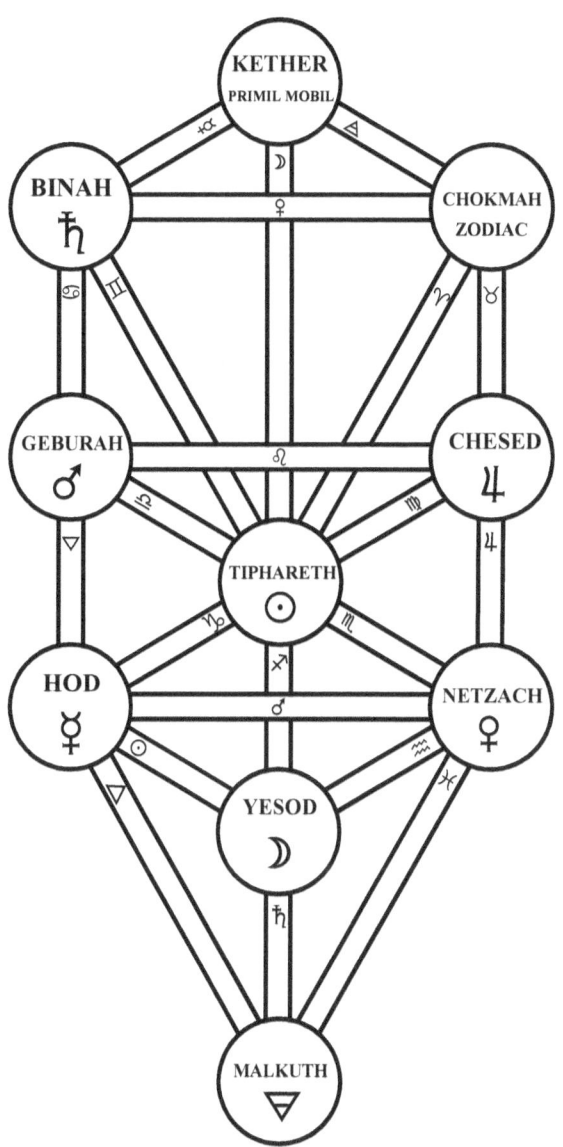

Diagram #26   Planetary Attributions and the Zodiac

THE HERMETIC QABALAH

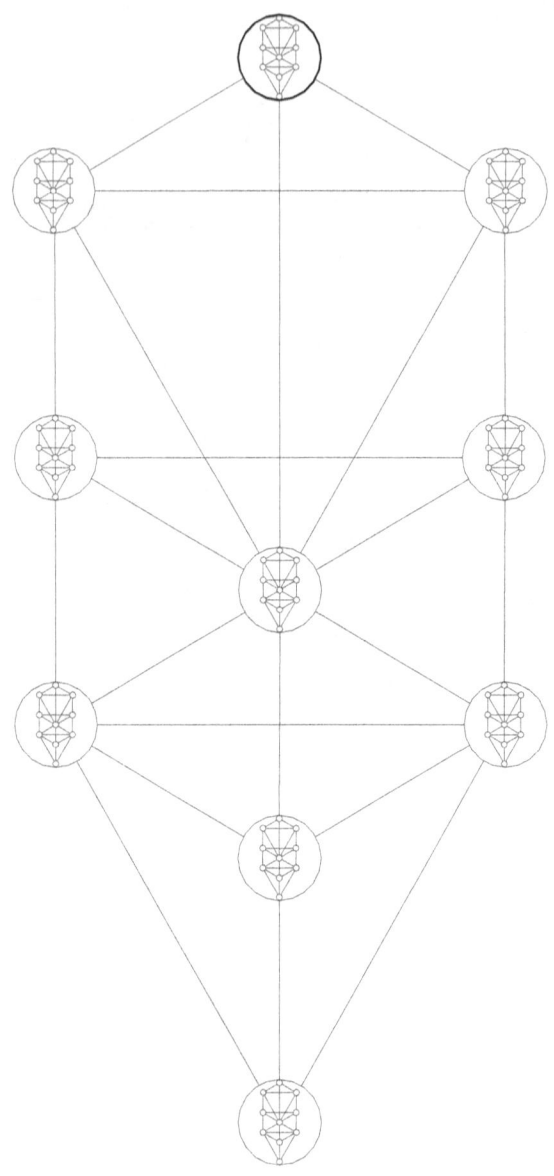

Diagram #27   The Tree in the Tree

THE HERMETIC QABALAH

The Pattern on the Trestleboard

This is Truth about the Self!

0. All the power that ever was or will be is here now.
1. I am a center of expression for the Primal Will to Good which eternally creates and sustains the universe.
2. Through me its unfailing Wisdom takes form in thought and word.
3. Filled with Understanding of its perfect law, I am guided moment by moment along the path of liberation.
4. From the exhaustless riches of the Limitless Substance, I draw all things needful, both spiritual and material.
5. I recognize the manifestation of the undeviating Justice is all the circumstances of my life.
6. In all things, great and small, I see the Beauty of the divine expression.
7. Living from that will, supported by its unfailing Wisdom and Understanding, mine is the Victorious life.
8. I look forward, with confidence to the perfect realization of the Eternal Splendor of the Limitless Light
9. In thought and word and deed, I rest my life, day by day upon the sure Foundation of Eternal Being.
10. The Kingdom of Spirit is embodied in my flesh

THE HERMETIC QABALAH

Select Bibliography

Butler, W.E. *Magic and the Qabalah,* Aquarian Press, London, 1964

Case, Paul Foster, *Occult Fundamentals & Spiritual Unfoldment* F.L.O., U.S.A., 2008

Case, Paul Foster, *Esoteric Secrets of Meditation & Magic* F.L.O., U.S.A., 2009

Case, Paul Foster, *The Book if Tokens,* B.O.T.A., Los Angeles, 1989

Clark Paul A. *The Threshold,* F.L.O., U.S.A., 1986

Clark, Paul A. *Personal Fulfillment & the Laws of Consciousness,* F.L.O., U.S.A., 2010

Coleman, Wade *Sepher Sapphires.* F.L.O., U.S.A., 2008

Collins, Mabel *Light on the Path,* Yoga Publications Society, Chicago, Ill, 2007

Fortune, Dion *The Mystical Qabalah* Williams & Norgate, Ltd. London, 1935

Gray, W.G. *The Ladder of Lights* Helios, Great Britain, 1968

Houston, Jean, *The Search for the Beloved*, U.S.A., 1997

Kaplan, Aryeh, *The Bahir,* Weiser, U.S.A., 1977

THE HERMETIC QABALAH

Mathers, S.L. MacGregor, ***The Kabbalah Unveiled,*** Weiser, U.S.A. 1977

Three Initiates, ***The Kybalion,*** Yoga Publication Society, Chicago, Ill., 1936

Valentine, Basil, ***Triumphal Chariot of Antimony,*** Kessinger Publications, U.S.A., 2007.

Yates, Frances, ***Occult Philosophy in the Elizabethan Age*** Routledge Classics, 2001

THE HERMETIC QABALAH

Index

Acolyte, 209

Akashic Library, 171

Akashic Records, 29, 68, 118, 186

Aleister Crowley, 108, 146, 269

Ancient of Days, 42, 234, 256, 257

Ann Davies, 111, 135

archetypes, 27, 33

Archetypes, 3, 25, 32

Aryeh Kaplan, 38, 39

Assiah, 29, 30, 32, 33

Astral Plane, 29, 48, 68

astral world, 102, 171

Attention gives life, 137

Atziluth, 25, 27, 28, 30, 147

Auriel, 28, 128

Baal ha-Daath, 71, 172, 182

Babylon, 36

Babylonian captivity, 2, 3

Bahir, 38

Beginning of the Whirlings, 42, 154

Binah, 17, 43, 53, 119, 120, 121, 124, 125, 129, 130, 132, 133, 135, 136, 137, 138, 141, 142, 146, 149, 201, 244, 245, 261, 267, 269, 279

Bodhisattvas, 121

Bohu, 25, 26, 27, 126

Book of the Dead, 7, 92, 93, 111

Brethren of the Rosy Cross, 121

Briah, 27, 28, 30, 33, 161

THE HERMETIC QABALAH

Bride, 48, 62

Buddha, 187

Calcination, 258

Carl Gustav Jung, 24

causal relationships, 77

Cause and Effect, 16

Chabad, 127

Chai, 193, 233

Chaiah, 143

chakra, 118, 155, 195

chakras, 84, 114, 173, 190, 233, 260

Chaldean Oracle, 52

Chasidim, 44

Chesed, 43, 44, 54, 107, 117, 118, 119, 120, 121, 122, 133, 228, 230, 231, 232, 239

Chokmah, 17, 42, 43, 52, 53, 119, 121, 124, 125, 130, 132, 137, 142, 143, 146, 147, 149, 150

Cholem Yesodoth, 48

Christ Consciousness, 45

Christian, 3, 35, 37, 39, 43, 59, 99, 100, 143

chyle, 236

Collective Consciousness, 179

Collective Subconsciousness, 67

Collective Unconscious, 171

Collective Unconsciousness, 29, 56, 67, 71, 80

Corpus Hermeticum, 7, 37

Correspondence, 9, 10, 21, 25

Cosmic Consciousness, 168

cosmic egg, 172

Cosmic Will, 107, 108, 111, 117, 120, 154, 155,

THE HERMETIC QABALAH

218, 219, 221, 239, 253, 259, 265, 280

Cosmic Womb, 43, 53

Cosmo de Medici, 37

Cube, 139, 140, 175, 190, 191, 195

Cube of Space, 140

Da'ath, 127, 128, 135, 229, 262, 269

Daath, 119

day-house, 109

Desire Force, 46

desirelessness, 46

Din, 44, 110

Dion Fortune, 39, 134

discovery of the first Matter, 150

Donald Duck goes to Math Magic Land, 82

Dr. James Henry Breasted, 93

Dweller on the Threshold, 92, 93

Egoic Triad, 107

Ehben, 95

Elemental Kingdoms, 102

Elysian Fields, 94

Emperor Marcus Aurelius Antonius, 38

Empty Room, 128, 135

enlightenment, 59, 85, 101, 124

Essene, 36

Eugene Emard, 155

Exempt Adept, 107, 118, 119, 121

Fez, 37

Fibonacci Series, 78

Fiery Intelligence, 147

Fire, 39, 49, 63, 88, 105, 114, 142, 147, 176, 178, 196, 228, 261

THE HERMETIC QABALAH

first-day awareness, 61

Flame alphabet, 36, 146

Fool, 164, 278, 280

foundation, 37, 44, 48, 63, 67, 79, 80, 81, 84, 146

Fraternity of the Hidden Light, 84

Freemasonry, 32

Gabriel, 178

Garden of Eden, 48, 62, 170, 228, 266

Geburah, 44, 45, 54, 107, 108, 110, 117, 120, 121, 133, 137

Gematria, 3, 26, 27, 36, 69, 136

Gender, 16, 17

Gnosis, 72, 124, 125, 128

golden mean, 78

Great Lies, 70, 77, 138, 145, 284

Great Sea, 43, 136

Great Work, 60, 75, 87, 113, 162, 171, 174, 191, 205, 221, 228, 235, 242, 244, 247, 250

Greater Adept, 107, 121

Green Lion, 236

Guph, 49

Hall of Judgment, 111

Hall of Osiris, 100

Hanged Man, 108, 143

Haniel, 119

Hermes Trismegistus, 7

Hermetic principles, 9

Hermeticism, 6, 9

Hierogamos, 113

Hierophant, 7, 100, 120, 208, 252, 253, 254, 265

High Priestess, 69

Higher Self, 49, 54, 55, 57, 71, 74, 81, 84, 87, 95, 98, 102, 105, 133, 135, 177, 178, 180, 182, 185, 188, 199, 205, 207, 208,

213, 214, 223, 232, 235, 258, 273

Hippocrates, 99

Hod, 47, 55, 56, 72, 74, 78, 79, 83, 84, 137, 176, 179, 181, 182, 184, 199, 218, 249

holographic, 6

Holy Guardian Angel, 33, 80, 81, 94, 99, 128

Holy of Holies, 135

Homo Illuminatus, 181

IHVH, 99, 143

Illuminating Intelligence, 150

imagination, 22, 28, 29, 70, 71, 81, 84, 86, 87, 112, 145, 155, 182, 186, 210, 211, 213, 240, 264, 280

Individuality, 43, 45, 80, 84, 87, 91, 95, 98, 102, 103, 105, 107, 117, 119, 149

Initiation, 72, 128, 162, 163, 167, 284

Ipsissimus, 154, 155, 270, 280

Isaac Luria, 37, 39

Islam, 99, 108

Jesus, 1, 59, 61, 74, 81, 85, 95, 99, 104, 105, 118, 121, 138

Johann Reuchlin, 39

Judgment of Maat, 100

Kabbalah Denudata, 25, 39

Karma, 94, 110, 111

Kat Stevens, 61

Kether, 10, 42, 48, 52, 53, 54, 56, 57, 69, 118, 119, 121, 124, 125, 130, 131, 132, 136, 147, 152, 153, 154, 155, 156, 157, 158, 163, 201, 229, 232, 256, 257, 267, 268, 272, 278, 279

King chamber, 100

THE HERMETIC QABALAH

King Scale, 162

Kingdom, 34, 48, 56, 57, 59, 61, 62, 93, 98, 100, 105

Knower of the Truth, 113

Kundalini, 114, 173, 176, 225, 241, 242, 266

Kybalion, 6, 9, 11, 20, 21, 63, 124, 263, 293

Law of Inner Causation, 14, 24

Law of Response, 76, 154, 248

Lesser Adept, 107

Lesser Mysteries, 58, 74, 84, 86, 92, 94, 209

Lie, 85, 109, 118, 196, 200, 201, 202, 214, 223

Life and Death, 62

Light in Extension, 98

Lightning Flash, 53, 56, 130, 153

Limitless Light, 42, 154

Limitless Substance, 118

Logoidal Consciousness, 46

Logos, 165, 180, 206, 254

Lords of Compassion, 44

Louie Claude de Saint Martin, 85

Love, 17, 27, 28, 45, 48, 88, 96, 97, 120, 121, 127, 133, 182, 191, 228, 229, 231, 232, 239, 271, 273

Magical Image, 99, 150

Magister Templi, 133

Magus, 144, 145, 146, 148

Malka, 59

Malkuth, 10, 28, 48, 49, 56, 57, 59, 60, 62, 63, 64, 66, 67, 72, 136, 155, 162, 176, 185, 229, 269

mandala, 42

Manipura chakra, 118

Manly P. Hall, 93

THE HERMETIC QABALAH

Manus, 165

Mara, 136

Mars energy, 109, 110, 112, 113, 114

Marsillo Ficino, 39

Masculine Pillar, 43, 142

Masonic, 100

Master, 40, 51, 71, 77, 117, 119, 121, 133, 134, 144, 149, 156

Master of Knowledge, 71

Materialism, 44, 77, 92, 284

Mediating Intelligence, 54, 57, 88

Meditation, 190, 192, 240, 257, 292

Melekh, 59

men and women of desire, 85

Mentalism, 9, 18, 19, 20

Mercury Center, 155

Mercy Seat, 135

Merkabah, 36

Merkavah School, 161

Messiah, 45

Mezla, 147

Minutum Mundum, 161, 162

Mithras, 99, 105

Mortality, 77, 92, 284

Moses ben Shem Tob de Leon, 39

Moses Cordavero, 37

Mysteries of the Kingdom, 59

Neo-Platonist, 35

Nephesh, 68

Neshamah, 43, 132, 136

Netzach, 46, 47, 55, 56, 81, 84, 85, 90, 120, 184, 185, 189, 228, 229, 249, 264

New Jerusalem, 62

THE HERMETIC QABALAH

night-house, 109

Nirvana, 46

One Ego seated in the heart, 109

Orpheus, 99

Osiris, 99, 105

Pachad, 44, 110

Palace of Holiness in the Midst, 140

path of return, 59, 128, 145

Path of Return, 77, 163, 164, 167, 176

Path of the Names, 39

Path of the Uniting Intelligence, 69, 119, 126, 127

Pattern on the Trestleboard, 34, 110, 118, 148

Paul Case, 176, 206, 218, 222, 233, 265, 280

Paul Foster Case, 39, 71

Perpetual Intelligence, 175, 177, 178

Personality Triad, 46

Philosopher's Stone, 114, 150

Philosophus, 84, 87, 88

Pi, 150

pineal gland, 156

Pineal Gland, 114

Polarity, 11

Powder of Projection, 156

power paths, 81, 155

Practicus, 74, 77, 181, 184, 185

Practicus., 181

Primal Point, 52, 130, 153, 154

Primal Will, 42, 75, 108, 118, 137, 145, 147, 149, 155, 285

Prostatic Ganglion, 114

THE HERMETIC QABALAH

Qabalah, 2, 3, 6, 10, 17, 19, 20, 25, 26, 35, 36, 37, 38, 39, 51, 59, 70, 94, 99, 108, 113, 114, 120, 124, 125, 130, 131, 133, 135, 136, 142, 153, 284, 292

Qebel, 3, 35, 120

Qoph, 26, 183, 185, 186, 187

Quantum Physics, 6

Queen Scale, 161

Rabbi Akiba, 38

Rabbi Nehunia ben ha-Kana, 38

Rabbi Simeon ben Jochai, 38

Radical Intelligence, 108

Raphael, 28, 119

Rashith ha-Galgalim, 154

Ratziel, 36, 39

Recepticular Intelligence, 120

Receptive Tradition, 39

red lion, 225, 242

Rhythm, 13

root of air, 132

root of fire, 130, 132

root of the power of water, 136

Root of the Power of Water, 132

Rosetta Stone, 42

Rosicrucian, 76, 100

rough ashlar, 32

Royal Road, 94

S.L. MacGregor Mathers, 39

Sacrificed God, 45

Safed, 37

Sakel Tahoor, 70

Sanctum Sanctorum, 135

Savasthana Chakra, 114

THE HERMETIC QABALAH

Saykel Oboah, 120

School of the Prophets, 36

secret seed, 70

Separation, 77, 85, 118, 284

Sepher Sapphires, 126, 292

Sepher Yetzirah, 170, 176, 191, 230, 242, 254

Serpent of Wisdom, 153

Seven Heavens, 68

Shamayim, 149

Shekinah, 135

Sherlock Holmes, 61

Shin, 26, 99, 175

singularity, 51, 52, 53, 130

Society of Martinists, 85

Solar Logos, 45, 98

Solar Plexus, 118

solve et coagula, 171, 213

Solve et Coagula, 88, 104

St. Francis of Assisi, 86

String Theory, 145

Sufi, 3, 35

Sulphur, 256

Sun-King figures, 105

Supernal Sephiroth, 53, 121, 124

Supernal Triangle, 53

Supreme Mysteries, 119, 123, 133, 135

Tartarus, 94

Tatwas, 78

Tav, 26, 138, 167, 170

Temple of Solomon, 62

Ten Luminous Emanations, 39

Tetragrammaton, 99, 143, 144

THE HERMETIC QABALAH

The 32 Paths of Wisdom, 167

The Big Bang, 51, 130

The Book of Tokens, 39

the *Egyptian Book of the Dead*, 111

the Emerald Tablet, 21, 69

The Greater Mysteries, 91

The Harp of Ten Thousand Strings, 48

The Kabbalah Unveiled, 39, 293

The Ladder of Lights, 126, 292

The Portal, 91, 92, 93

The Serpent of wisdom, 161

The Tower, 113

The Zohar, 38, 56

Theurgy, 19, 31, 32, 254, 281, 282, 283

Third Order, 78, 102, 119, 121, 133, 134

Thirty-two Paths of Wisdom, 38

Thoth, 7

Thousand Petal Lotus, 155

Tiphareth, 45, 48, 49, 54, 57, 62, 69, 79, 95, 98, 99, 100, 102, 103, 104, 106, 107, 109, 117, 120, 128, 133, 149, 190, 199, 221, 223, 232, 239, 246, 247, 249, 251, 252, 268, 279

Tree of Life, 2, 3, 17, 19, 28, 33, 40, 41, 42, 51, 52, 53, 64, 69, 79, 84, 92, 104, 126, 127, 129, 132, 136, 159, 160, 161, 162, 164, 170, 176, 193, 203, 214, 228, 229, 240, 249, 250, 264, 267, 268, 272, 282, 284, 286, 288

Triad of the Kings, 117

Triumphal Chariot of Antimony, 87, 293

THE HERMETIC QABALAH

True and Invisible Order, 74

Unfinished Temple, 133

Unity, 27, 42, 69, 75, 113, 126, 138, 181, 182, 271, 284

Unknown Philosopher, 85

unreserved dedication, 86

vibration, 11, 12, 30, 48, 110, 125, 145, 146, 148

Vibration, 11

vital soul, 48, 74

Vital Soul, 67, 68

Void, 26, 153, 182, 271

volitional energy, 110

Warrior, 117

Water, 178

Wisdom, 17, 36, 42, 47, 52, 56, 63, 70, 96, 97, 120, 143, 145, 146, 148, 149, 150, 153, 156, 159, 160, 161, 162, 172, 175, 191, 193, 207, 229, 233, 247, 263, 265, 269, 270, 272, 273, 276, 279, 285, 291

Wise and Foolish Builder, 95

Yah, 70, 71, 143, 144

Yeheshuah, 99

Yekhidah, 155, 262, 267

Yesod, 48, 55, 56, 65, 67, 69, 70, 72, 73, 74, 77, 171, 172, 179, 181, 182, 189, 190

Yetzirah, 28, 30, 32, 33, 38, 40, 67, 127, 140

Zelator, 60

THE HERMETIC QABALAH

THE HERMETIC QABALAH

Dr. Paul A. Clark is the Steward or visible head of the Fraternity of the Hidden Light, a worldwide esoteric initiatory Order in the Western Mystery Tradition. For several years he studied personally with the Reverend Ann Davies, former Prolocutor General of Builders of the Adytum. Paul left B.O.T.A. in 1982 to found the Hidden Light as an Aquarian Age incarnation of the Ancient Esoteric Orders. He is the author of a number of books and courses on subjects of the Hermetic sciences. Paul spends much of his time lecturing on esoteric topics throughout the world. He currently resides in the Los Angeles area of Southern California.

For more information on the Hidden Light

lvx.org

THE HERMETIC QABALAH

www.ingramcontent.com/pod-product-compliance
Lightning Source LLC
Chambersburg PA
CBHW031234290426
44109CB00012B/283